THE KILLER COOKBOOK

EDITED BY CARO RAMSAY

UNIVERSITY OF

DUNDEE

Discovery Press
An imprint of the University of Dundee

MILLIONFORAMORGUE.COM

First published in Great Britain in 2012 by

Discovery Press
University of Dundee
DD1 4HN

Illustrations © Steve Carroll
www.stevecarroll.co.uk

ISBN: 978-1-8458699-9-1

British Library Cataloguing-in-Publication Data
A catalogue record for this book is available on request from the British Library.

Design and typesetting by Joby Catto
www.anti-limited.com

Printed and bound in Great Britain by Bell & Bain Ltd., Glasgow

Thank you so much

Sue x

Contents

Foreword
Professor Sue Black

Foreword

I am the luckiest person on the planet. I have the enviable position of being able to combine my two greatest passions in life - human anatomy and forensic anthropology - into a job for which I get paid. I get to do this in a Centre where I am surrounded by the most experienced team in the world and in a University that is progressive and reactive. Whilst what we do is extremely serious, we manage to cram a huge volume of laughter and camaraderie into our working day. So when the University sets what seems an almost impossible task to achieve – raise a million pounds for a mortuary – I simply couldn't be in a better place to have a go at making it work. In our Centre, literally nothing is impossible and with a staff that have been weaned on Blue Peter and Dad's Army, if we can't beg for it, borrow it, or steal it, then we will make it out of sticky-backed plastic and a wire coat hanger.

Ingenuity becomes a way of life in our field and we just love a challenge. Fortunately for me, as I have progressed through these unchartered waters of fund raising, I have been blessed by the support of so many like-minded people who have recognised the importance of what we are trying to achieve and understood that sometimes you simply have to follow the eccentric route if you want to succeed. We have had some great ideas from our authors on how to raise money through unusual means – I particularly loved the idea of auctioning the name of a corpse in a forthcoming crime novel. Their ingenuity and support has been humbling and heart-warming and so to the latest idea – a killer cookbook. You might think that food and my job are not easy bed partners, but there is nothing gets you more starving hungry than a full day's work in a cold mortuary or out on a crime scene up to your armpits in muck and mire!

Thank you for buying this book and for contributing to the Million for a Morgue campaign. I hope you really enjoy all the recipes donated by our contributors. Why not try them all out and if it all goes seriously wrong… maybe I will see you earlier than you anticipated! Enjoy - because life is short and we are all a long time dead.

Thank you for buying
this book. It is
hugely appreciated.

Sue. October 2012.

Professor Sue Black

Introduction
Caro Ramsay

Introduction

Editing a cookbook is a strange occupation for a crime writer who lives in a house with no kitchen and does not care. My great advantage is that I have many friends in low places, friends who are strange crime-writing types, friends who lurk in the darkness of the human mind...

Writing a novel is a solitary occupation. For me there are rewrites and rewrites of 440 typed A4 pages, hours of typing, fighting with post-it notes, trying to resist googling myself again with only the snore of the faithful hound for company.

Every so often we are allowed out to crime festivals to meet each other and mingle with the public under the watchful eye of an agent or an editor. Most writers jump at the chance to be on a panel and this year I was given the honour of moderating an international panel at Crimefest in Bristol. One of my topics for discussion was how your country of origin aids body disposal (a popular topic with the audience). The New Yorker stuck the body in a dumpster. In Botswana it is easier to dump the body on a route where a hyena will stumble over it and then call his pals to join in the buffet. The speed at which a hyena can strip a body is frightening. In Venice, just throwing somebody in the canal will give them severe stomach issues that can prove fatal if it suits the plot. I was musing about dropping bodies into Scottish lochs and letting the pike have a nibble. The Swedish crime writer simply said, "I would feed him one of my sandwiches as I am the worst cook in the world, then dump the body in the Stockholm archipelago". I would like to point out that Anders got his friend, an award-winning chef, to contribute his recipes for this book. So you are safe.

Professor Sue Black was holding a reception for the Million for a Morgue Campaign at Crimefest that evening. We got talking about pike and hyena and she gave me that strange look that I'm sure she gives most crime writers. It's a look that says, you have a sick and perverted mind.

But we are nice with it.

I did my forensic medical diploma at Glasgow Uni, and recall Dr John Clark giving us a lecture about the mass graves at Srebrenica in 1995, talking us through the nuts and bolts of identification of the 3000 victims. That process that is still ongoing. I'm sure we all recall the aftermath of the tsunami in 2004. My colleague at work was on holiday in Thailand at the time and had been chatting at breakfast with her husband about going on a hill walk that day or going on the scenic coastal railway. They decided on the hill walk. The train disappeared, no survivors.

Funds from the sale of this book will help Sue build a Thiels morgue at Dundee, which will help train those who stand on the front line of international disasters and help put a name to victims and return them to their families.

Enjoy the book! Enjoy the humour! Enjoy the recipes! And thank you for supporting this good cause.

Caro Ramsay

Caro Ramsay

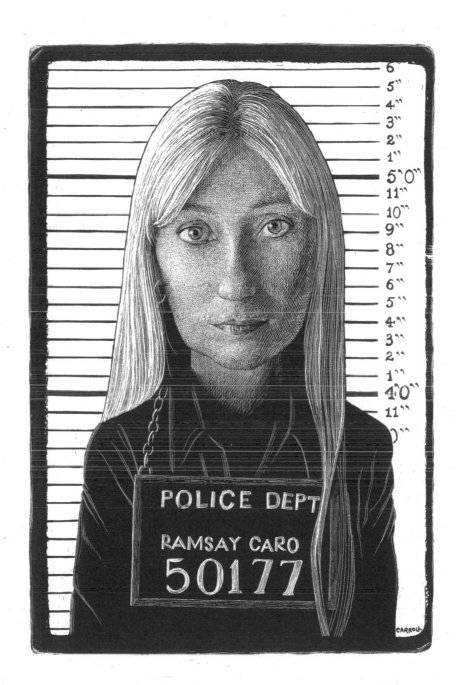

Aperitifs

Tom Black's Killer Margarita

Professor Sue Black

My husband makes the best Margarita and at the time they don't taste as if there is any alcohol in them at all. They are frighteningly easy to make and scarily easy to drink. After one there seems to be no problem in the world that you can't overcome and after two, some rotter has stolen your legs! I have never dared three.

Serves 2

Ingredients

- 1 part fresh lime juice
- 5 parts Gold Tequila
- 2 parts triple sec
- 2 parts good quality lime cordial

Execution

Place two triangular Margarita glasses in the freezer for a few minutes.

Fill a cocktail shaker with ice and add all the ingredients. Shake well for about twenty seconds and pour into the chilled glasses. Serve with a slice of lime on the edge of the glass.

Peter James and I have two things in common. Well, three if you count crime writing. We both have a house full of dogs and we both live in old houses with a resident ghost. But I bet his ghost is not called Agnes. I know he has a background in film production, but I think he would make a great Bond villain. They missed a trick there; every time I hear him speak I can imagine him saying... "Oh, you think so, Mr Bond?" before doing something despicable and dastardly with a hint of sadistic humour.

Peter's cocktail could be added to the Vespers and the Bradfords. All shaken, not stirred!

Caro

The Peter James Vodka Martini Writing Special

This is my 6pm tipple that acts as rocket fuel to kick off my evening's writing. One sip of this, music blasting from my speakers, and I'm typing away happy as Larry!

Serves 1 author

Ingredients

1 cocktail shaker
Ice cubes
1 proper, crystal martini glass of decent quality. No other drinking vessel can be substituted.
1 bottle Grey Goose vodka (or your preferred brand - this is mine!)
1 bottle Martini Extra Dry
1 lemon
or
4 plain olives, pitted
1 cocktail stick

Execution

Half fill the cocktail shaker with ice. Fill the martini glass three quarters full with vodka. Using the cap of the Martini Extra Dry bottle, tip two measures of Martini into the glass. Pour the contents of the glass into the shaker and secure the top carefully.

Now you have a choice. A twist or with olives. My taste alternates!

With a twist:

Cut a lemon in half. Peel a thin strip of rind three inches long and drop into the glass. Then cut a wedge from the lemon, make a slit in the centre, and run this all the way around the rim of the glass on both sides.

With olives:

Spear four olives with cocktail stick and place in the glass.

Give the cocktail shaker a hard shake, remove cap and pour.

Enjoy! But just remember the caveat: "Ladies, beware the dry martini, have two at the very most… for with three you will be under the table… and with four you will be under your host."

Soups, Starters and Salads

STUART MACBRIDE

Stuart MacBride says on his website that he wrestles bears professionally.
Well, you can't argue with that as he lives in Aberdeen. He once injured his
back doing a reverse overhead pile driver on a grizzly but the grizzly replied
with a triple back flip sulko with full half-twist peloton. While Stuart was
pretending to be injured, I was pretending to be an osteopath. He took his
shirt off to show me his wounds and I have been on medication ever since.

No conversation between Stuart and I ever makes sense.
But somehow the world looks better that way...

Caro

Mushroom Soup

Something strange began to happen to me the moment I went full time as a writer: I became a much bigger man. By which I don't mean that I became important, or special, or even taller... actually, I've been getting shorter for the last fifteen years. Shorter and rounder. For some God-forsaken reason I'm slowly turning into a pasty bouncy castle with a beard. A podge.

A sexy podge, but a podge nonetheless.

I never used to be - I used to be slim and fit and a bit of a hottie - it's the writing that's done it. Back when I worked full time for THE MAN I'd get back home from work and sit down to indulge in my dirty secretive hobby: writing. So that's all day sitting in an office, followed by all night sitting in the study making up lies about people who don't exist. Not the most active of lifestyles, but at least back then I was getting a bit of exercise walking to the shops for lunch. Now the only things that get exercised are eight fingers and the lump of gristle between my ears.

Worse yet, I came up with a new hobby: cooking. Well, I couldn't keep writing in my spare time, could I? That would just be silly. You don't take up professional dentistry, spend all day traumatising people by drilling holes in their teeth, and then go home and start hacking away at your neighbour's mouths with a hammer drill, do you? Well, not unless you want to feature on the evening news in a couple of years' time. No, you find yourself a decent wholesome hobby, like drinking heavily, or line-dancing dressed up like Barney the Dinosaur.

And as my purple Tyrannosaurus Rex costume is still in the dry-cleaners after an unfortunate semolina-related mishap, I took up cooking. It started out small, just the occasional pot of mince and tatties... I thought I could handle it. I could stop any time I wanted. Then I started dabbling with more exotic things like stews, roasts, and, to my eternal shame, fondue. And then I tried the hard stuff: soup.

POLICE DEPT
MACBRIDE STUART
50181

28

What could be more distracting than soup? It's like sex in a pot... Well, maybe not sex, not unless you're into scalded genitals and finding bits of diced carrots in your intimate crevasses. But there's something strangely hypnotic about the alchemical nature of combining random stuff you find in your fridge and transforming it into SOUP!

I suppose soup is a strange obsession for someone who writes police procedural thrillers that often get described as gorier than shoving a rabid weasel down a haemophiliac's trousers. But there you go; we all have our dark secrets. And the darkest of my dark secrets is the infamous MUSHROOM SOUP.

When my editors decided to take a punt on my first book, Cold Granite, they asked me to write a small bio to go with the photo of the thin tall bloke on the cover. So I did:

"Stuart MacBride has scrubbed toilets offshore, flunked out of university, set up his own graphic design company, worked for some really nasty marketing people, got dragged into the heady world of the Internet, developed massive applications for the oil industry, drunk heaps of wine and created the perfect recipe for mushroom soup..."

That bit at the end has got me into more trouble than pretty much anything else. As soon as I realised I was getting more emails about the damn soup than the damn books I dropped the soup thing from the bio, but by then it was too late. Four years later and I'm still getting mushroom-soup-related queries. Seriously, these people aren't asking about recurring themes, metaphors, or the importance of cannibalism in modern crime fiction. No, they want to know about bloody soup.

Serves 4

Ingredients

150g dried porcini mushrooms
Thumb-sized lump of butter
400g mushrooms, sliced really thinly
Loads of fresh thyme, finely chopped
85g leeks, finely chopped
2 cloves garlic, mashed
1¼ litres full-cream milk
2 slices of bread, or a stale roll
150ml double cream
1 palmful of fresh parsley, finely chopped
Salt and freshly ground black pepper

Execution

Start off by rehydrating the dried porcini mushrooms in a small bowl of hot water. They'll take about twenty minutes to plump up and soften. It might seem like an odd amount, but it's about half a little packet.

Next, melt the butter in a soup pot, chuck in the sliced fresh mushrooms and season with salt and pepper (the thinner you slice them the more surface area they have to ooze out mushroomy goodness). Sweat down the mushrooms until they're soft and all the moisture has come out of them. Then add the chopped thyme, leeks, and garlic. Let them heat up in the mushrooms for a couple of minutes, then pour in the milk and bring it up to a very gentle simmer. Thyme and mushrooms go incredibly well together, trust me on this...

Tear or slice up your bread and stick it in a heatproof jug. Chuck in the rehydrated porcini and a couple of ladles of the warm mushroomy milk, then liquidise it all up with a hand blender. If you don't want to throw out the soaking liquid, make sure you strain it before you add it to the soup or it'll be full of grit and sand and bits of dead bugs.

Blending it all up should give you a jug of very tasty, intensely mushroomy moosh: tip it back into the pot. Add the double cream, chopped parsley, then check for seasoning – mushrooms and cream are both sponges for salt and pepper, so don't be shy about it – then serve.

If you're feeling all summery, leave out the bread and substitute a good quality, free-range chicken stock for the milk. It won't be quite as rich, but it'll be a lot lighter. You could add a slug of brandy or a couple of glugs of white wine to the mix, but for God's sake make sure you add them after the rest of the liquid or the mushrooms will soak up all the booze. This might seem like a good thing, but it'll just make them all bitter and nasty. Like an OAP with a septic leg and a colostomy bag full of second-hand chilli. You really want to be eating that?

(This recipe first appeared on the excellent www.murderati.com blog.)

IAN RANKIN

There's a funny thing about Scottish men (not Ian specifically - in general, I mean). They can have no idea where the hoover is, need a sat nav to find the washing machine, yet will pride themselves on being able to make a 'good pot of soup'. These soups tend to be made with any spare veg that are lying around as leftovers.

I can remember soup like this being made by Granny with a ham bone going in with whole potatoes along with all the other ingredients. It was left to simmer for what seemed like a fortnight, then the ham and (now cooked) spuds were removed and eaten as a main meal. The rest of the 'soup' did us the following day... and the day after that.

Caro

Vegetable Soup

This is one of the few things Rebus can cook.

Execution

Chop and fry a medium onion and a couple of cloves of garlic in some vegetable oil (in a good-sized pot). After a couple of minutes, start adding chopped veg – anything you like – carrots, potatoes, leeks, cabbage, sprouts, turnip. You don't need to be fussy about quantities.

Stir the pot while frying. You want the veg slightly browned/golden/softened.

Boil a kettle of water and add enough to the pot to cover the contents. While it bubbles away, add a pinch of salt and pepper (to taste) and a good sprinkling of dried mixed herbs. Reduce the heat and cook until it looks like soup.

Done.

ROSLUND † HELLSTRÖM

I have to confess that I am a huge fan of these two. They have published six books in the Ewert Grens series. Three Seconds and Cell 8 are the most recent ones to be translated into English. And as I write this, one of them is getting the Hollywood treatment. The books are not being published in chronological order in the UK: you can keep tabs on them at www.roslund-hellstrom.com.

It was on a panel with Anders Roslund and Michael Sears that the idea of this cookbook came about. I pointed out that poor Ewert never ate anything decent; compared to Michael Sears' character Kubu (see the Bobotie recipe on p.80). Here is what Anders has to say about it:

Caro

Ewert Grens, Detective Superintendent at the Stockholm City police, lives in his office. He sleeps, works, eats on his worn out sofa or desk. He doesn't eat much: he drinks seas of black coffee in plastic mugs and buys cinnamon buns from the vending machine in the corridor. That's it. Sometimes he celebrates with a forgotten sandwich hidden in a plastic cover. Maybe this reflects the two authors – not much cooking and eating, well, whatever we can find.

So, when we were asked for the tenth time to give a seminar at my hideaway – a small cottage in a jungle on a lovely and isolated island called Arnö, located in the Swedish lake Mälaren – we finally said yes on one condition: if my next door neighbour would agree to cook and serve for the evening. We of course reckoned he would turn us down.

He didn't.

My next door neighbour is Christer Lingström, one of the most famous chefs in Sweden. In 1985 he won the Swedish "Chef of the Year", then he was awarded one Michelin star in 1992 and another in 2000. His restaurant Edsbacka Krog was the first Swedish restaurant ever to receive a second star.

To arrange this event and make it perfect, Christer asked me the very obvious question: 'What does Ewert Grens eat?' He got the cinnamon bun answer. Therefore, and for one night only, the most prestigious chef in Scandinavia created a special Arnö Soup, based on ingredients you can find on this small island, and a special Ewert Gren's Sandwich.

The seminar with Roslund & Hellström was a success. People drove through the sunny summer night from the closest towns Strängnäs and Enköping, and even all the way from Stockholm. We are still arguing if the attraction was the books - or the food.

Soup de Arnö

Serves 4

The ambition is to capture the aromas of the forest – and for this you'll need:

Ingredients

500g wild mushrooms, e.g. chanterelles
1 onion, finely chopped
50g butter
2 tbsp wheat flour
300 – 400ml chicken or vegetable stock
300ml cream
200g smoked bacon, diced
Salt and some white pepper

Execution

Preheat the oven to 200C.

The secret behind this soup is to start off frying the mushrooms and onion in butter. Then you roast them in the oven until they're fairly dry.

Move the fried and roasted mushrooms out of the oven and into a pan. Sprinkle the flour in and stir. Add the stock and cream and cook for about forty minutes, then season with some salt and white pepper to taste. Blend the soup smooth.

Fry the bacon. To remove excess fat, let the bacon rest on some kitchen roll after it's done.

Pour the soup into deep plates, sprinkle with bacon and serve.

Ewert would possibly enjoy this together with a glass of Madeira.

Ewert Gren's Sandwich, or Water & Bread
(when out of cinnamon buns)

Serves 4

Ingredients

200g ham
100g pickled cucumbers
50ml mayonnaise
100ml crème fraiche
Any nice white bread
Fresh Horseradish
Salt and freshly ground black pepper

Execution

Start by cutting the ham into small squares, then chop the pickles and mix it all together with mayonnaise and crème fraiche. Season with salt and pepper to taste. Serve on a slice of white bread topped off with some freshly grated horseradish.

KATHY REICHS

Kathy Reichs writes the Temperance Brennan novels and the TV series <u>Bones</u> is based on her work. She also continues to work as a forensic anthropologist, helps to teach FBI agents to detect and recover human remains, and is a consultant for the Laboratoire de Sciences et de Medecine Legale for the province of Quebec. Phew.

The weather often plays a big part in her books, the temperature often dropping way, way below zero or snow drifting feet high. Not something British Rail could cope with easily.

Caro

Chilled Avocado, Lime and Coriander Soup with a Shrimp Salsa Island

Serves 4 - 6

Ingredients for soup

2 ripe avocados
2 tbsp sour cream
1 cup (250ml) double cream
1 cup (250ml) whole milk
3 tbsp fresh coriander, chopped
3 tbsp fresh lime juice
1 tbsp fresh lemon juice
½ tsp salt
Pinch of ground black pepper

Ingredients for shrimp salsa island

For the base of the island you will need wonton or Chinese dumpling wrappers. These you can usually find in the oriental section of your supermarket or in a Chinese market.

2 or 3 roasted yellow tomatoes (you can sometimes find these roasted already in oil in specialty food markets or roast your own – see below; if yellow tomatoes are not available you can use red ones)

4 – 6 wonton wrappers (depending on how many people you're feeding)

120g cooked small prawns

¼ red pepper, finely chopped

¼ yellow pepper, finely chopped

1 tbsp fresh coriander, finely chopped

2 tsp fresh lime juice

1 lime, cut into wedges

Execution

Cut the avocados in half; remove the stone and scoop out flesh with a soup spoon. Place in a food processor or blender with the rest of the ingredients, and process until smooth. Chill until you're ready to eat.

If you're roasting your own tomatoes, preheat the oven to 160°C. Take two or three fresh yellow tomatoes and cut in half. Squeeze lightly to remove the seeds. Rub with olive oil and salt lightly. Place cut side down on an oiled baking sheet and roast in the oven thirty to forty-five minutes or until tomatoes have almost dried out.

Take the wonton wrappers and fry them flat on both sides in vegetable oil until golden brown and crispy. Leave to cool on some kitchen paper.

Mix together all the remaining ingredients apart from the lime wedges, and season with salt and some freshly ground black pepper.

To serve, pour the soup into individual chilled bowls, then place a crispy wonton or dumpling wrapper in the middle of each serving. Balance a tablespoon of the shrimp salsa on top and garnish with a sprig of coriander and a lime wedge.

Spicy Tuna Tartare on European Cucumber Slices Topped with Honey Wasabi Sauce

Ingredients for the tuna tartare

700g sushi quality tuna

3 tbsp Sriracha (Thai garlic chilli sauce available at speciality stores)

2 tsp ginger juice (peel and grate an inch or so of fresh ginger, then squeeze into a bowl)

2 tsp toasted Japanese sesame oil

2 ½ tsp salt

2 cucumbers, sliced

Ingredients for the honey wasabi sauce

3 tbsp dry wasabi powder

2 tbsp honey

250ml sour cream

Execution

For the tuna tartare, either:

Cut the tuna into small pieces. Toss with remaining ingredients. Place the mixture in a food processor and pulse till the mixture begins to hold together.

Or:

Chop the tuna by hand into very tiny pieces that hold together in a ball. Mix in the other ingredients.

For the wasabi sauce, whisk all ingredients together till just blended – don't over mix or the sauce will get too thin.

To assemble the final dish, place a teaspoonful of the tuna mixture on the centre of a cucumber slice. Top with a small dollop of honey wasabi sauce (this is easy if you put the sauce in a squirt bottle).

Russian Stuffed Aubergine

Serves 4

Ingredients

2 medium aubergines
Olive oil
100g pecorino cheese
100g walnuts
100g rocket
80g parmesan shavings

Execution

Slice the aubergines thinly on the diagonal to make a dozen long oval slices. Fry in batches in hot oil and set aside to cool. Chop cheese and walnuts to breadcrumb consistency and mix together. (It's best to do this in an electrical chopper but you can do it by hand.) Place a generous teaspoon of the cheese and nut mix on an aubergine slice and roll it up. Serve garnished with rocket and Parmesan shavings and a light dressing of olive oil.

Skaagen Toast

Peter James

This is a Swedish starter. The Swedes are blessed with having some of the world's best seafood, especially prawns. Depending on budget, accompany with a fine white Burgundy, or a Muscadet sur Lie.

Serves 6

Ingredients

1 ripe but still firm avocado
3 tbsp mayonnaise
3 tbsp crème fraîche
1 lemon, cut into quarters
6 slices medium-sliced white bread
10g red onion, finely chopped
1 pot Swedish caviar (or red caviar)
300g peeled prawns
A few sprigs of fresh dill, finely chopped
Some watercress to garnish
Salt and freshly ground black pepper

Execution

Slice the avocado thinly. Mix the mayonnaise and crème fraîche together and season lightly with salt and pepper and a squeeze of lemon.

Remove the crusts from the bread, then toast it lightly and cut into four squares per slice.

Spread a layer of the mayonnaise/crème fraîche mix on the toast. Then layer on top avocado slices, more mayonnaise and crème fraîche, then the onion, then the caviar, then the prawns.

Sprinkle dill on top and garnish each one with a sprig of watercress.

Tess has now retired from her medical career to write full time. No wonder, with her books selling twenty-five million copies world-wide. She is best known for her Rizzoli and Isles series which is now on the telly starring Sacha Alexander as Maura Isles the forensic pathologist (you might also know her as Kate Todd in NCIS). Maura is 'The Queen of the Dead.' Detective Jane Rizzoli, the girl who hunts monsters, is played by Angie Harmon (Abby Carmichael from Law and Order).

Caro

Spicy Chinese Chicken Salad

Serves 8

Ingredients

110g dried Chinese bean thread noodles (also known as rice sticks, they're available in most supermarkets in the Asian foods section)
Groundnut oil for deep-frying
1 head iceberg lettuce, shredded fine
4 chicken breasts, roasted, cooled, and shredded
6 spring onions, sliced fine
20g sliced almonds
1 handful fresh coriander, chopped

Ingredients for dressing

3 tbsp soy sauce
4 tbsp sesame oil
1 tbsp sesame seeds
2 tsp rice wine or white vinegar
Cayenne pepper to taste

Execution

Fry the bean thread noodles: heat two inches of groundnut oil in a wok or saucepan until it starts to smoke. Fry the bean threads a few strands at a time (they are wiry while uncooked and you'll need to pry apart and break the nest of tangled noodles). Once in the hot oil, they should puff up within seconds. Remove as soon as they are puffy and drain on paper towels.

Toss together the shredded lettuce, chicken, fried bean threads, spring onions, almonds and coriander. Whisk together the dressing ingredients in a small bowl, adjusting the spiciness by adding as much cayenne pepper as you like. Pour over the salad, and toss again before serving.

Kate is one of those authors that put us mere mortals to shame – she's on book seventeen as I write this, will probably be on book eighteen by the end of this sentence and twenty by the time she has made the Chicken a la Christie! She is the author of two crime series – one, featuring Devon-based DI Wesley Peterson, blends history and modern day crime, while the other is set in spooky North Yorkshire and features DI Joe Plantagenet. Her latest novel, The Cadaver Game, is out now in paperback.

Caro

Sesame Chicken a la Christie

Sesame Chicken a la Christie is easy, quick to make, and delicious enough to serve to friends washed down with a couple of bottles of wine. The ideal recipe to make after a day spent fighting crime in print!

Ingredients

3 tbsp coarse grain mustard
1 tbsp clear honey
3 tbsp sesame oil
2 or 3 chicken breasts cut into strips
1 ripe avocado
1 bag of green salad
2 tbsp vinaigrette
2 tbsp sesame seeds
Salt and freshly ground black pepper

Execution

Mix together the mustard, honey, and sesame oil in a large bowl and leave the strips of chicken to marinate in the mixture for an hour or two. Stir-fry in a wok until the chicken is cooked through. Slice the avocado, toss with the salad and vinaigrette. Add sesame seeds to the wok and cook for one more minute until the seeds begin to change colour. Pile the hot sesame chicken and juices over the salad and serve.

ALINE TEMPLETON

Aline grew up in the fishing village of Anstruther on the east coast of Scotland, not far from St Andrews. The memories of that beautiful scenery and the close community inspired her to set the Marjory Fleming series in a place very like that – rural Galloway, in the south-west of Scotland.

Conversations between Aline and I never get too far before we start talking about our favourite subject – dogs and their love for life, sticks, and all things silly. We agree that the best dogs are those who engage enthusiasm before brain.

Caro

Bloody Mary Tomatoes

As DI Marjory Fleming is a notoriously bad cook, she can't cope with anything that demands more than stirring ingredients together. This is the only recipe she makes with confidence, and possibly slightly too much vodka. The last time she had people in for drinks, two of the unwitting guests were breathalysed on the way home.

Ingredients

250g baby plum tomatoes
200ml Vodka
1 tbsp sherry
A few drops of Tabasco
Salt and freshly ground black pepper

Execution

Score a cross on the base of each tomato. Put in a plastic box, cross uppermost. Whisk together all the other ingredients and pour over. Put in the fridge for forty-eight hours.

Drain and bring back to room temperature before serving.

Warning: these pack a serious punch!

LINDA STRATMANN

Linda writes the Frances Doughty Mysteries, a series of whodunits set in Victorian Bayswater featuring a young female sleuth. I have seen her many times at festivals and am always impressed by the fact she has made her detective so different. Not pretty, not pathetic, she just gets on with the job. 'Miss Doughty? The girl who won't take no for an answer!'

Caro

Store Cupboard Tapenade

When I am not writing about crime I am cooking, though I have to reassure people that my interests in murder and food are not connected in any way! I like to invent my own recipes and here is one that I devised one day when I wanted to eat tapenade but didn't have the classic ingredients to hand so made it using what I had in the store cupboard. It was so successful I have been making it this way ever since.

Ingredients

60g stuffed green olives

20g black olives (I used the dry black ones so had to slice the flesh off the stones to get 20g olive flesh)

1 small (80g) tin of tuna in spring water, drained

Juice of half a lemon

½ tsp coarse grain mustard

1 tbsp tomato puree

1 tbsp olive oil

Freshly ground black pepper

Execution

Put all the ingredients in a food processor and whizz to a thick paste, stopping and pushing the mixture down with a spatula if necessary. Depending on the juiciness of the lemon you may need to add a little more juice or even a teaspoon of water to get the right consistency.

Serve as a dip with celery sticks or on crackers.

Enjoy!

Main Courses

JEFF LINDSAY

Jeff Lindsay is scared of me, officially. As he writes the Dexter books you would not think that he would scare easily but hearing my Glaswegian accent in the confined space of a lift in a hotel in Bristol had him spooked. I think Billy Connelly tells a story of something similar happening to him in New York, that our Glaswegian Gatling delivery can appear threatening to slow-talking Americans. Jeff is a comedian, blues singer, and musician. He told me once the he is married to the third international Hemingway...

Caro

Cody's Quick Chicken Curry

This recipe is quick and easy, and kids like it. It's also a good way to get children used to the idea of spices, which comes in handy later when you want to make Dexter's Kind of Hot Chilli.

Any good, mild curry powder will work; I am from Miami, so I use Badia brand, but most spice sections will carry something that works...

Serves 4-6, or 2 teenagers

Ingredients

2 boneless, skinless chicken breasts

1 tbsp extra virgin olive oil

½ an onion, finely chopped

1 tbsp minced garlic

2 tbsp mild curry powder

2 tbsp soy sauce

30g golden raisins

2 eggs

2 large tbsp smooth peanut butter

1 head broccoli, chopped into florets

Execution

While you heat a large pan to just past medium heat, chop the chicken into small cubes. Put olive oil in the pan and add the onion. Stir occasionally until the onion just starts to turn translucent.

Add the garlic and stir once. Put in the chicken, then add the curry powder and then the soy sauce, and fry until the chicken is browned, stirring often to stop it sticking. I always add a little water to help the spices mix evenly with the chicken.

When the chicken is evenly browned, toss in the raisins. Push it all to the side of the pan and break in the eggs. Scramble them until firm and then mix together with the chicken.

Push the chicken and egg mixture to the sides again and add the peanut butter to the pan, along with three or four tablespoons of water to thin it. Stir in with the chicken until everything is evenly coated. Toss in the broccoli florets. Pour in a little more water and cover the pan. Cook for eight to ten minutes, stirring occasionally, until broccoli is al dente.

Remove lid and serve over rice.

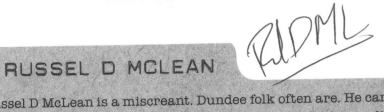

RUSSEL D MCLEAN

RIDML

Russel D McLean is a miscreant. Dundee folk often are. He can be seen at Crime events running around in black, with a microphone, climbing over seats and accosting ladies, like Anneka Rice on a mission to deliver Black Magic chocolates. He works for a well known chain of book shops as well as being no mean writer in his own right, or should that be in his own write? His books have been described as 'awesomely dark'. He shares a pastime with many Scottish men: 'blethering shite!' He shares a passion for garlic with Michael Malone (see page 56). Indeed, they seem to be having a face-off here...

Caro

Le Poulet au Canaille, or Dead Man's Breath

This is one of those recipes that might make your jaw drop. Because no one seems to believe me when I tell them what the centrepiece of this old French peasant dish is. So let me make this perfectly clear: when I say thirty cloves of garlic, that is not a misprint. I really do mean three-zero.

The recipe is an old favourite of mine. I found the basis for it in a recipe book by Edouard Du Pomaine, and while I may vary here and there from his instructions, the recipe is remarkably simple and astoundingly tasty. If you don't mind a bit (or possibly a lot) of garlic breath the next morning…

Serves 4

Ingredients

30 (twice fifteen) cloves of garlic (this is recommended for four people, although given my weakness for garlic, I still tend to use the same amount even for two people. Your mileage may - and probably will - vary)
10 shallots
Olive oil
Butter (or margarine if you really must)
Chicken pieces (2 per person, preferably on the bone, so thigh is ideal)
A fine, dry white wine
Salt and freshly ground black pepper

Execution

Prepare by removing the garlic cloves from the bulb but do not remove the skin. Leave your garlic in its skin. You'll see why later. You should also finely (or, as I do, crudely) chop those ten shallots. But beware: I have found they're worse than regular onions for making you weep.

Use a casserole dish with a wide base for this one. A Le Creuset or similar is ideal. It will be heated on the rings of your cooker, not in the oven. First of all heat your olive oil in the dish, and add a large dollop of the butter. Allow it to melt. Put in your chicken and allow it to brown on both sides (this should take about five minutes). While this is happening, add copious amounts of salt and pepper.

When your chicken is brown, reduce the heat a touch, and put in all that sliced shallots and garlic. Give this about ten minutes, until they are beginning to soften. Again, salt and pepper.

Now comes the fun part. Remember that fine, dry white wine? Open it. Pour a glass for yourself. You deserve it.

Then take another glass and pour that into your mixture. Let it simmer and then cover the pan and cook for around forty minutes. You may want to check on it every so often and perhaps have a wee guddle (that's a technical term for basically stirring things around).

After forty minutes, uncover your casserole. Let it bubble away and over about ten minutes the liquid should reduce.

If you desire, you can serve with some boiled potatoes (dripping with butter, of course) or cabbage, but keep any sides very simple indeed. This is a peasant dish, after all. When serving, do not put the casserole directly on the plate. Instead take the casserole dish to the table and place it on a heat-proof mat in the centre (this, as my dining room table can tell from an accident many years ago, is essential). Everyone then helps themselves. Now, remember I told you to leave the skins on? There was a reason. When you eat the garlic, squeeze it between your teeth so that the by now soft centre of the garlic squirts into your mouth. Discreetly spit the skin onto your fork and put it to the side of your plate. This, with a mouthful of the soft shallots and the tender flesh of the chicken is a taste experience to be savoured.

But just remember the next morning that you may have to talk to people with one hand covering your mouth.

MICHAEL MALONE

Who needs this amount of garlic? Has Burns country become a haven for vampyres or something? Scary. Michael is scary. So are his books. Great but scary.

Michael J. Malone hails from Ayrshire, is a published poet, a regular reviewer with www.crimesquad.com, and works in publishing. He wants his tombstone to read that he never ate enough Mars Bars. Blood Tears is his first novel.

Caro

Chicken with Forty Cloves of Garlic

Yeah, you read that right. Forty. Four-Oh.

Ingredients

1 chicken (plucked etcetera – 'cos the feathers tickle the back of your throat)
1 tablespoon olive oil
20g butter
40 garlic cloves, unpeeled
3 thyme sprig thingys
1 fresh bay leaf
310ml chicken stock
185ml white wine (what you do with the rest of the bottle is entirely up to you, but cooking time is one hour twenty minutes. Just sayin')

Execution

Preheat your oven to 200°C.

Season your bird, inside and out, with salt and ground black pepper. Then make like your favourite fictional serial killer and tie the legs together. But use string, not duct tape.

Heat your oil in a large, heavy flameproof casserole dish over a high heat. Add butter. Add chicken to butter. Brown chicken on all sides. (Its wee tippy-toes will be difficult to brown so you can skip that.)

Remove chicken. Add garlic (remember – forty cloves), thyme, and bay leaf. Stir. Return chicken to the casserole, breast side up. Add stock and wine and bring to a simmer. You know, like your missus does when you KEEP LEAVING THE TOILET SEAT UP.

Cover the casserole. With the lid, silly. And cook in the oven for forty minutes. Then remove the lid and cook for another fifteen minutes or until the chicken is cooked through. Remove chicken and half the garlic cloves. Go on, count 'em. Twenty. Cover chicken loosely with foil to keep it all warm an' cosy.

Place your (large, heavy, flameproof) casserole dish over a medium-high heat. Press the remaining garlic with a potato masher to extract the flesh. Extract the flesh. (Oooo, shivers.) You can provide your own sound effects. Bring this sauce to the boil and cook for about five minutes or until reduced to 185ml. Then pass this liquid/pulp/extracted flesh through a fine sieve to extract as much of the flesh (Oooo, shivers) as possible. Now stir in the garlic you removed earlier.

The resulting sauce can be drizzled over the chicken that you are about to carve with your favourite knife. Wait. You don't have a favourite knife? That's really just me? Serve with mashed potatoes and green beans. Or don't.

Serve

Eat. Note: It is alleged that garlic cooked in this manner will have a more subtle flavour. Let us know how much of a social outcast you become after eating this, wontcha?

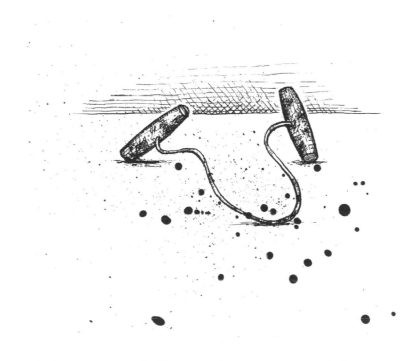

PETER GUTTRIDGE

Peter Guttridge is a very clever and talented chappie: he is a novelist, critic, writing teacher and interviewer at all sorts of literature festivals and events. He has also just stepped down from his eleven-year role as crime fiction critic of the Observer newspaper. He is universally hated on the first night of Crimefest Festival as he is the quiz-master and he makes the questions very hard. (He once gave our team a point for spelling our own names right. We were so bad we were in danger of getting nil point!). He is then universally adored on the final afternoon by volunteering for the Mastermind quiz where he has to sit in 'that' chair, under 'that' spotlight, while Maxim Jakubowski says, 'I've started so I'll finish'.

Peter has been known to answer questions in French just to confuse the audience.... or hide the fact that he doesn't know the answer.

You can tell that this recipe has a kind of 'hang about the kitchen, fling in some wine, drink some wine, chill in the kitchen, drink some more wine' feel about it.

Enjoy!

Caro

Peter's Chicken Breast

Execution

The lentils are green and (in my case) usually undercooked but simmered with fennel seed, finely chopped celery, onion and (if you're so inclined) pancetta in half a bottle of red wine. Lots of black pepper, of course.

The chicken breasts are skinned, opened up and stuffed with black olive tapenade/paste then held together with string. They're cooked on the top of the stove in olive oil first then simmered in milk. Once cooked, they're sliced into these medallions of white chicken and black olives (which have infused the chicken) and served on that bed of lentils.

Looks great, tastes great.

DEAN CRAWFORD

Dean is an author whose work is scarily real. Science faction mixed up with crime fiction in tightly-written thrillers. He knows such a lot about science and technology, he keeps himself right at the front of all kinds of innovation and if you don't believe me just check out the guy's website!

Caro

Barbeque Chicken Stir Fry

I'm not what you'd call a gourmet chef by any standards, but I created this criminally good little number when I was living alone in a rented flat with barely enough money to get by, struggling to finish yet another novel and begin the heartbreaking rejection process of finding an agent. Fortunately it worked with that novel and I got my agent and publishing deal (with Simon & Schuster/Touchstone USA). So this dish has a special significance for me. I've also tested it on friends and family and they actually loved it!

Anyway, here it is.

Execution

Take a perfectly healthy chicken. Murder it.

Abduct several innocent peppers and onions and keep them hostage in a dark place. Forcibly kidnap a pack of medium noodles and likewise detain them against their will.

Slice the chicken into chunks and marinade in thick BBQ sauce for an hour or two. If you're really sadistic, let the peppers and onions watch while you do it.

Put the remains of the dead chicken, in its sauce, into the oven for half an hour at around 200°C.

While the unfortunate chicken is cremating, force your peppers and onions to watch as you heat a frying pan of seething oil and also boil some water in a saucepan.

One by one, slice your peppers and onions into small pieces.

Throw the peppers and onions into the frying pan. They may squeal a bit but don't worry, they're not getting out of there alive. Stir-fry their remains for about ten minutes.

Hold the (by now) trembling noodles over the boiling water for a few, terrifying moments, then drop them in with an evil laugh. Boil them alive for four to five minutes.

When the suffering is over, serve the noodles onto the plate first, then the fried onions and peppers on top, and finally add the nicely barbequed chicken.

Voila!

JOHN GORDON SINCLAIR

John Gordon Sinclair, the actor, has now turned his hand to crime writing with his first novel, Seventy Times Seven. He is probably best known for playing the gangly teenager in Gregory's Girl. I confess I remember him best for being on Wogan. I think it must have been St Andrew's Day or a Burn's Night edition as he was asked to taste a few haggis (haggi? haggises? I suppose it depends if there are many of the same species or one each of many different species? Like fish and fishes?) The bold Terry asked him for his opinion. When John reached the veggie haggis he had a tentative mouthful and exclaimed, 'That tastes like something that came out the back end of a dog'. I wondered then, as I wonder now, how he knew that.

Caro

Pomegranatastic Melonmatic Crispy Duck

Ingredients

2 bottles of chilled beer

½ or whole crispy aromatic duck depending on how many people you're serving (Sainsbury's do the best). If you're a loner or have no friends get the whole duck anyway: it's so tasty you'll wish you'd made more.

2 tbsp groundnut oil

200g bean sprouts

Heaped cup of cashew nuts

1 large clove of garlic (or two small), crushed and chopped.

1 chopped red chilli (optional)

2 tbsp sweet soy sauce

2 tbsp Thai fish sauce

2 pomegranates, deseeded

Handful of fresh coriander, chopped

Handful of Thai basil, chopped

½ iceberg lettuce, finely shredded

½ watermelon, diced

Execution

Drink one of the chilled beers then prepare the duck as per instructions on the packet and set aside.

The next bit only takes a few minutes so do it just before you remove the duck from the oven.

Heat the groundnut oil in a wok or large frying pan until hot enough to land you in A&E if you spilled it on yourself.

Flash fry the bean sprouts, along with the cashew nuts, garlic, chilli, fish sauce, and sweet soy sauce, for no more than three minutes. At the last second throw in the pomegranate seeds (just to warm, not to cook).

Remove from heat.

Then and only then mix in a generous handful of both the chopped coriander and the Thai basil.

It's now time to drink the second beer.

Arrange the iceberg lettuce and diced watermelon on a shallow serving dish.

Shred the duck on top, then tip the contents of the wok over it and serve.

JEFFERY DEAVER

Jeffrey looks like an undertaker, he says this himself. Or a mortician. Or somebody who lives in an old house where the doors creak ominously and a single crow sits on the gatepost. He could sit in his dark room in a turret and look at his bone collection.

However, he is in fact a lovely warm and very funny human being, a good singer as well as one of the best crime writers on the planet.
For the pub trivia fans, he also wrote the James Bond novel, Carte Blanche.

Caro

Bone Collector Recipes

Don't you just love bones? I know I do. The shape, the feel... the sound! So much fun. And, guess what? You can also find them in some very tasty recipes. Here are three of my favourites.

Chicken Wings

Serves 4 - 6

Ingredients for marinade

1 clove of garlic, crushed
180ml dry white wine
½ tsp Worcestershire sauce

Ingredients for chicken

25 chicken wings
125g plain flour
½ tsp cayenne pepper
½ tsp salt
¾ tsp freshly ground black pepper
170g butter, melted
125ml hot sauce of your choosing

Execution

Combine the marinade ingredients in a plastic bag and add the wings. Refrigerate overnight.

Remove the wings from the marinade and pat them dry. Put the wings with the flour, cayenne pepper, salt and black pepper in another plastic bag. Shake to thoroughly mix.

Place the wings on an oiled baking sheet and refrigerate for one hour.

Preheat oven to 200°C.

Combine the melted butter and your hot sauce in a small bowl and whisk together. Brush generously on the wings, top and bottom.

Bake for twenty minutes, then turn the wings over and bake for another twenty to thirty minutes until cooked through.

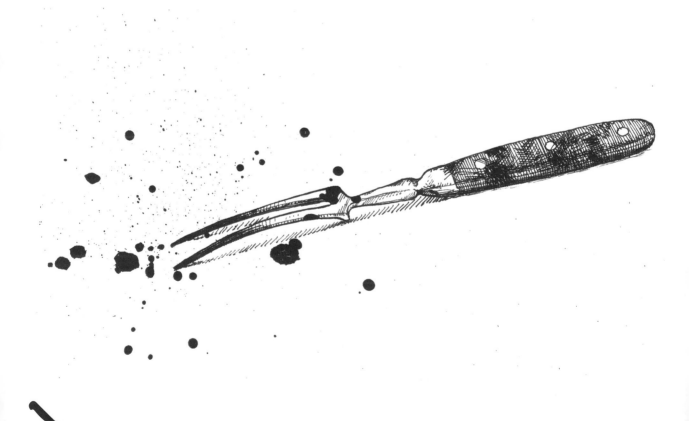

Stuffed Pork Chops

Serves 4

Ingredients

4 thick pork chops, with bone
55g butter
2 tbsp finely chopped onion
4 tbsp dried cherries, chopped
4 tbsp raisins, chopped
½ baguette, cubed and toasted
60ml chicken stock
¼ tsp dried sage, crumbled
¼ tsp dried rosemary, crumbled
2 tbsp olive oil
Additional melted butter
80ml kirsch
Additional chicken stock
Additional chopped cherries and raisins for garnish
Salt and freshly ground black pepper

Execution

Preheat the oven to 175°C.

Cut slits into the pork chops to the bone.

In a saucepan, heat the butter over a low to medium heat (it burns easily!) and slowly cook the onions, cherries and raisins until soft.

Take the pan off the heat and add the bread cubes, chicken stock, herbs and a pinch of salt and pepper, and stir well.

Stuff the mixture into the slits in the pork chops, and secure with toothpicks.

In an ovenproof cast-iron pan, heat the oil and brown the pork chops. Then brush them with some of the additional melted butter and bake, uncovered, for thirty to forty minutes until cooked through.

Remove the chops to a warm serving plate.

Deglaze the pan over low heat with the kirsch (careful, it can catch fire!) and additional chicken stock. Pour this over the chops and garnish with additional chopped cherries and raisins.

Short Ribs

Serves 4

Ingredients

1.8 kilos beef short ribs, cut crosswise into pieces 6 – 8cm long
3 tbsp extra virgin olive oil
2 medium onions, chopped
2 tbsp plain flour
1 tbsp tomato puree
560ml dry red wine
1 tsp each dried thyme, rosemary, oregano, and sage, crushed
1 bay leaf
2 cloves of garlic, crushed
750ml beef stock
Salt and freshly ground black pepper

Execution

Preheat oven to 175°C

Salt and pepper the ribs. Heat the oil in a large casserole and brown the ribs slowly in batches so that they're thoroughly browned. Set them aside.

Drain off most of the oil and drippings, leaving about three tablespoons in the pan. Brown the onions. Add the flour and tomato puree and cook, stirring constantly, for several minutes until uniform in texture.

Return the ribs (and any juices from plate) to the pan. Add the wine, bring to the boil and then lower the heat to simmer.

When the liquid is reduced to about half, add the herbs and garlic.

Add stock and bring to boil, then cover and transfer to the oven.

Bake until the ribs are very tender - about two and a half hours.

Take the ribs out of the pan and put on a serving plate.

Skim the fat from the remaining liquid and bring to a fast boil to thicken on the hob, then strain onto the ribs.

ZOE SHARP

Zoë Sharp wrote her first novel when she was fifteen. She created Charlotte 'Charlie' Fox – the no-nonsense ex-Special Forces-turned-bodyguard heroine of her best-selling crime thriller series – after receiving death-threat letters as a photojournalist. Her work has been nominated for the Edgar, Anthony, Barry, Benjamin Franklin, and Macavity Awards in the United States, as well as the CWA Short Story Dagger. She blogs regularly on her own website, www.ZoeSharp.com, and on the acclaimed group blog, www.murderati.com.

Caro

Slow-Cook Lamb (to the Slaughter)

I'm not a huge carnivore, but my favourite meat has to be lamb – apart from the fact it can so often be tough and chewy, not to mention very fatty. This recipe, however, allows you to make use of the cheapest cuts and turn them into the kind of melt-in-the-mouth meal you can eat yourself sitting in front of the TV on a cold winter's night, or serve to dinner party guests.

I think this recipe must be almost unique in the collection in that it contains no booze. If you really must, you can add a splash of sherry to it, but as a boring teetotaller I have to leave that bit out.

Ingredients

1kg or so of lamb
An onion, roughly chopped
Additional veg to suit, roughly chopped
Enough lamb stock to cover
2 tsp cornflour
Several cloves of garlic
2-3 tbsp light soy sauce
1 tbsp honey (runny is easier, but set will do)
1 tbsp balsamic vinegar (or red wine vinegar or whatever vinegar you have)
½ tsp ground ginger
½ tbsp Marmite (optional but recommended)
Gravy granules (optional)
For this you also need a slow cooker or crockpot

Execution

Take however much lamb you happen to want to cook (OK, you get the idea, this is going to be a very imprecise recipe). Trim off the biggest lumps of fat, but you don't need to be too fastidious about this. You can brown it in a frying pan first if you really want to, but it's not compulsory.

Throw the meat into your slow cooker/crockpot. I've done this with either a complete half-shoulder or chopped up lumps of stewing meat. The recipe works well with either. The only limitation really is the size of your crockpot and the number of guests. If it's for two, you can get several meals out of it at least.

Roughly chop the onion and throw that in right at the beginning as well, plus any other veg that benefits from long slow cooking, like carrots. It depends what's hanging around in the bottom of the fridge and looks in need of using up.

Add enough lamb stock – made with one stock cube is fine – to cover the meat. If you haven't got lamb stock cubes, use beef or veg ones. Add a couple of heaped teaspoons of cornflour mixed up in a little cold water, plus whole cloves of garlic (quantity really depends on taste and who you have to speak to the following day, plus whether it's face-to-face or on the phone), the soy sauce, honey, vinegar, a smidge of ground ginger, and a generous glob of Marmite. I know this last ingredient sounds weird, but it adds a really good meaty flavour. I've fed this to people who really do not like Marmite, and they still love the recipe.

You probably don't tend to need to add any extra salt because of the soy sauce.

If you've left plenty of time – around six hours – before you want to eat, set the crockpot on 'Low'. If you want to eat sooner – four hours or less – set it to 'High' for the first hour, then turn it down to 'Low' for the remainder of the cooking time.

Now go and write something!

About an hour before dinner-time you really need to get rid of some of the excess fat that's melted out of the meat. You can either do this by carefully spooning it off the surface or pouring the whole lot into a separator jug, in which case you'll need to remove the meat and veg into a bowl with a slotted spoon before you transfer the remaining liquid into the jug. (Just FYI, I let the fat cool and then set it in the freezer before hanging it out for the birds.)

If you've used a piece of meat with the bone in – such as a half-shoulder – this is also a good opportunity to remove the bones and any lumps of fat or gristle that haven't melted. (Identifying them anatomically is optional at this stage.)

That done, pour the liquid back into the crockpot (if you went for the separator-jug method). Put the meat and veg back into the liquid. Taste for seasoning. Add additional cornflour or gravy granules to thicken it a little more if you like gravy you can eat with a knife and fork, plus throw in any extra veg that doesn't require so much cooking time, like mushrooms.

Now go back into the study and edit whatever it was you wrote while the thing was cooking.

Serve with whatever takes your fancy – baked or boiled standard or sweet potatoes, or rice, peas, green beans, garlic bread, crusty bread, etc.

Leave what's left to cool, at which point you can usually get rid of a bit more fat from around the edges with a spoon. Then you can either freeze the whole lot or reheat the next day.

This really is a perfect writer's meal. It doesn't really matter how long it cooks, or when you eat it, so if inspiration has stuck and you're madly scribbling, another half an hour simmering away is not going to do it any harm.

Enjoy!

MARTIN WALKER

For more than three decades Martin Walker has been an international correspondent reporting from all over the world, but now he writes really great crime fiction. He's a bit of a Francophile, especially when it comes to cuisine and cultural history. Both play a prominent role in his latest crime novel featuring Bruno Courreges. I wonder if the author is the official wine taster for the character, all in the name of research of course.

Caro

Bruno's Marinated Lamb Chops with Mint and Monbazillac Sauce

Bruno is the hero of the five 'Bruno' novels set in the Perigord region of France. A local village policeman who tends to solve crimes through his local knowledge, often to the frustration of the scientific specialists of the Police Nationale, Bruno is a passionate cook and gourmet who loves the local foods and wines. This is his version of a classic local dish, best served with a good Bordeaux or a fine Bergerac or Pecharmant red. Chateau de Tiregand Millesime 2005 or a good Pomerol would be perfect.

Serves 8

Ingredients for the marinated lamb

8 good-sized lamb chops
2 tbsp olive oil
8 cloves of garlic, crushed
4 sprigs of fresh thyme
4 sprigs of fresh rosemary
One glass Monbazillac sweet white wine from Bergerac.

Ingredients for the sauce

1 large bunch of fresh mint leaves, finely chopped
Juice of 1 lime
115g roasted pine nuts
1 large red onion, finely chopped
2 cloves of garlic, finely chopped
2 large tbsp olive oil
Another glass of Monbazillac

Execution

Mix the lamb chops with the marinade ingredients and leave overnight if possible but at least for two to three hours.

Mix together all the ingredients for the sauce in a bowl and put aside. Then, either in a grill pan or on a barbecue, grill the lamb chops for no more than five minutes on each side, depending on thickness of meat and how well done you want it. Allow to rest for five minutes and serve with the mint-Monbazillac sauce.

Bruno usually serves this with fresh asparagus and/or new potatoes, boiled and served with butter and ground black pepper.

Bon appetite.

LAURA WILSON

Laura is another extremely talented mega being. As well as being a multi award-winning historical fiction writer, she is the crime reviewer for The Guardian. She is also one of those writers who likes daft dogs, which is obviously the main topic of conversation when we meet – usually at those parties where you run out of hands – wine glass in one, tiny sandwich in the other when someone important is introduced. Formally.

Caro

Carpetbag Steak (with Oysters)

For anyone who needs to impress a carnivore, this is the perfect recipe as it enables you to wield sharp knives, turn up the gas, and generally whack a lot of flesh around the kitchen. It is a favourite of Roxy Beaujolais, who runs the marvellous Seven Stars pub, conveniently situated just behind the Royal Courts of Justice in Carey Street, London.

Roxy recommends serving this with soufflé potatoes, but as these are beyond my limited culinary abilities, I usually do roast potatoes and a green salad as an accompaniment.

Serves 4

Ingredients

A big squeeze of garlic puree
45g butter
8-10 oysters, cut in half if large
Handful of fresh parsley, finely chopped
4 fillet steaks, each 4-5cm thick
1 tbsp chopped fresh chives (optional)
Salt and freshly ground black pepper

Execution

Put the garlic puree and the butter in a small pan and heat gently. Add the oysters, sautéing until golden and beginning to crisp, then stir in most of the parsley. Turn off the heat.

Cut a big pocket in the side of each steak and fill with the sautéed oysters. Pan-fry the steaks on a hot skillet or in a frying pan. Dish up, spooning the remains of the garlic butter over the steaks, and sprinkling the remaining parsley on top, and, if you wish, the chives. Season and serve.

Alex lives down the road from me so we often car-share to events. It's not the first time we have missed a turning or gone round the same roundabout twice as we are too busy devising murder most foul to pay any attention to where we are going. I think she is in her element with one hand cooking her monkey glands on the Aga and the other hand cooking up dastardly plots on her iPad.

Caro

Monkey Gland Steak

Forensic tip: run cold tap when peeling onions to prevent tears contaminating the scene.

These are neither made from monkeys or glands but are certainly not for the vegetarians amongst us!

Serves 1

Ingredients

125ml brown vinegar
3 tbsp Worcester sauce
125ml tomato ketchup
1 onion, finely chopped
3 cloves
½ tsp prepared French mustard
Thick Rump Steak
Butter or oil
Salt and freshly ground black pepper

Execution

Combine the vinegar, Worcester sauce, tomato ketchup, chopped onion, cloves and mustard' and marinade the steak for at least thirty minutes. Fry the steak in a little oil or butter in a hot frying pan. Heat the left-over marinade in a separate pan and cooked till reduced by half. Serve with chips, salad, green peas or whatever you fancy.

CRAIG ROBERTSON

I can vouch for the fact that this man has a black pudding addiction. He needs help.

Caro

Human Black Pudding with Pan-Fried Scallops and Apple

No one who knows me will be remotely surprised that I've chosen a recipe with black pudding in it. I love the stuff and have travelled across Europe in search of the perfect plate of pud. I've seen it being made in Scotland, Ireland, France and Austria, and eaten it in Belgium, Germany, Italy, Spain and Slovakia.

It's made from blood for goodness sake! What self-respecting crime writer couldn't love a dish made from blood? For this particular recipe, I've chosen to go with black pudding made from human blood. I know what you're thinking... too much effort. But it's actually much simpler than you'd think.

The dish is very much like the classic French boudin noir – but with a twist. The French version is made of one third blood, one third fat, and one third onions. My version is more tartan noir than boudin noir, hence the human blood. Not human fat though, that would be disgusting.

Execution

You will need three plastic buckets, each containing equal portions of blood, fat and chopped onions, plus a funnel, a length of intestine and a large pot. Mix the blood, fat and onions together (a word of warning: human blood thickens slightly faster than pig's blood so make sure you keep stirring it or else it will congeal and you don't want that), season to taste, then pour the mixture through the funnel into the intestine. It is entirely a matter of personal choice whether you use human or animal intestine but the latter is generally easier to get hold off and much less fiddly.

Keep the intestine moving as the blood mix enters it to avoid lumps or twists, coiling it as you go. Once it is full, tie off the end and drop the coil into a pan of hot – not boiling – water and simmer for about twenty minutes. Et voila! Le boudin tartan noir.

If you are too lazy to bother making it from human blood then my recommendation would be either the fine ready-made black puddings of either MacLeod & MacLeod of Stornoway or Ramsay's of Carluke.

For the rest of the dish, simply melt a little butter or oil in a medium-sized frying pan and flash fry the scallops for about a minute on each side. Grill or fry the black pudding for a similar amount of time; ideally it will be crispy on the outside and moist inside so that you can still savour the tang of the blood.

To serve, slice up a green apple, or perhaps a pink lady, and arrange on the plate. Place a piece of black pudding on the apple, then a scallop on top of that.

Here's a bonus tip! Get an apple corer and carefully remove a small circle at the heart of one of the black pudding rings. Do the same with a slice of apple and pop the apple circle into the centre of the black pudding. You now have a rich, delicious piece of black pudding with a crisp, sweet heart. Do not discard the cored piece of black pudding as that would be a mortal sin, pop it on top of a scallop instead.

Every dish needs an accompaniment but personally I couldn't recommend any of those vegetable things that I hear people are eating these days. Instead I would advocate a liberal, yet not excessive, pouring of HP Guinness Sauce. If you feel the need to drink, I'd suggest a glass of Shiraz or a pint of double chocolate stout would go with it nicely. Bon appétit!

Craig Robertson

ADRIAN MULLER

Adrian Muller is a co-director of Crimefest, the international crime fiction convention held annually in Bristol. It was at Crimefest that the topic of food, or lack of it, in crime fiction came up on a panel that I was moderating.

That evening Professor Sue Black was holding her reception for The Million for a Morgue campaign, and I said something to the campaign co-ordinator, Emily Dewhurst, about crime writers and their use of food in books and then the discussion started...

Adrian knows everything and everybody in crime writing and anybody who has been to Crimefest knows what a jolly (drunken) time is had by all!

Caro

Sauerkraut with Chorizo Mince (served with mashed potatoes)

Ingredients

400 – 500g beef mince

Oil or butter

200 – 250 g chorizo, cubed

810g jar Sauerkraut, drained

150ml crème fraîche or sour cream

Ground paprika

Execution

Preheat the oven to 200°C. Brown the mince in a frying pan with a little oil or butter. Add the cubed chorizo and cook for a further five minutes. Drain the sauerkraut and squeeze out the remaining juices. Cover the bottom of an ovenproof dish with enough sauerkraut to just cover the bottom. Follow this with a layer of the browned mince and chorizo mix, and continue doing so there are four or five layers. Make sure that the last layer is sauerkraut, then spread the crème fraîche or sour cream on the top. Sprinkle lightly with some ground paprika and put in the oven to heat through and brown the top. Serve with mashed potatoes and red or white wine or Dutch gin.

Sally is another renaissance woman. Not only a crime writer but a sculptor, a poet, and also a renowned artist. Her husband is also a painter. Her sixth chiller, Cold Remains, is out now, as is her noir French thriller Malediction. Sally was born in South Glamorgan, Wales, but is often found in France, soaking up the atmosphere. She is a font of very creepy stories, very creepy indeed.

Caro

Baked Sausages in Gravy

Here's a recipe which is sooo easy and which was given to me by a South African friend...

Ingredients

2 packs of pork or Cumberland sausages
4 onions
Potatoes (allow two per person)
Pack of small tomatoes
4 peppers (not chilli!)
Gravy - enough to half cover the above when laid out in a baking tray

Execution

Preheat the oven to 180°C.

Prick the sausages and place them in a baking tray. Slice the onions and add. Quarter the potatoes and add. De-pip, slice the peppers and add. Add tomatoes. Add the gravy.

Cook on middle shelf of oven for about one and a half hours.

Bon appetit!

MICHAEL STANLEY

Michael Stanley is two people who write as one. (One is Michael and the other is Stanley, funnily enough). They are both South African by birth but set their books in Botswana. The books are full of life and sunshine and humour and star the great detective, Kubu. (That's his nickname, it means hippo.) It is fair to say that Kubu is rather fond of his grub. By book four, the creators put him on a diet, and he didn't like it!

Caro

Bobotie (South African Curried Minced Lamb or Beef Casserole)

Ingredients

1 slice of bread
750ml milk
900g minced lamb or beef
1 medium yellow or white onion, chopped
1 – 2 tbsp curry powder
1 tbsp brown sugar
1 tsp salt
½ tsp freshly ground black pepper
60ml lemon juice
4 eggs
150g seedless raisins
40g slivered almonds
1 cooking apple, grated
Several bay leaves

Execution

Preheat the oven to 150°C.

Put the bread into a bowl containing all the milk. Let stand. Lightly brown the meat in a frying pan, breaking up any chunks. Transfer to a large casserole dish with a slotted spoon.

Fry the onion in the fat left in the frying pan until translucent. Don't burn it!

Add the curry powder, salt, sugar, and pepper. Cook for two minutes, stirring. Add the lemon juice and cook for three more minutes. Pour over the meat.

Take bread out of milk and squeeze it out over the bowl. Put the bread in the casserole with the meat.

Add raisins, almonds, and apple to the meat mixture, then break in two of the eggs. Combine. (I use my hands to do this because it feels great and I can lick my fingers afterwards!)

Pack the mixture down in the pan. Push a few bay leaves into the meat, then beat the remaining two eggs with the milk and pour on top. Bake in the oven for 45 minutes.

Serve hot over rice, with chutney on the side. Leftovers are great hot or cold. Also leftovers can be put in pita bread with sour cream or used as a filling in an omelette. Yummy.

Spaghetti Carbonara

Russel D Mclean

Most recipes for Carbonara seem to involve an awful lot of faffing about with cream and mushrooms and all sorts of fiddly little moments. I am a very basic cook. I like my recipes simple but delicious. (The same way I like my crime novels, in fact!) I also have an allergic reaction to mushrooms so tend to leave those out. This recipe for Carbonara can easily be achieved in fifteen to twenty minutes, which makes it ideal if you don't want to waste any time.

Serves 2

Ingredients

Spaghetti
1 egg
Parmesan cheese
Bacon (I allow two slices per person but it's very much a judgement call)
Salt and pepper (but of course)

Execution

I am going to assume you know how to cook spaghetti. That's the best place to start. Kettle on, boiling water in pan, spaghetti in pan. Cover and cook for ten minutes. I also find that a splash of olive oil and salt in the water seems to make a difference to taste and stops the spaghetti sticking together.

While the spaghetti is cooking, crack your egg in a dish and mix in lots of grated parmesan and salt and pepper. Beat the mixture thoroughly. By hand.

Once you've done this, fry your bacon (sliced/cut with scissors/whatever your preference) in a pan until you're happy with it.

Drain the spaghetti and put it back in the pan but do not return it to the heat. Throw in the bacon (along with the oil you cooked it in) and mix. Then pour in your egg/parmesan mix and stir thoroughly. The mixture will be heated by the spaghetti and the bacon. If you do this on the heat the egg tends to scramble and you don't really want that.

Serve. Preferably with garlic toast (see below).

Garlic Toast

Making garlic bread is finicky and time consuming. When you're on a deadline you don't want to waste all that time, so here is a quick one I got from my dad.

Ingredients

1 clove of garlic
Bread (preferably a baguette cut open or a thickly sliced crusty loaf - sliced supermarket bread really doesn't work)
Olive oil
Salt

Execution

Toast your bread on both sides in the grill. Try not to burn it (this is my usual mistake). Bring it out and place on your plate. Take your garlic (de-skinned) and rub it across the top of the toast several times so that the garlic coats the bread. Dribble over some olive oil. Sprinkle salt. Rub the garlic across a few more times. Serve.

DANGER
RISK OF DEATH!

MARK BILLINGHAM

Mark is another one of these polymaths: actor, scriptwriter, stand up comedian, crime writer... and now he's adding cooking to his repertoire. Acting-wise, you might know him best for playing Gary in Maid Marion and Her Merry Men. Obviously he writes the Tom Thorne books, played recently by David Morrissey in the TV series. There is a rumour that if he ever went on Celebrity Mastermind his specialist subject would be looking out the window.

Caro

My Recipes: A Mission Statement

Some people say that whatever your physical age, you remain another age altogether in your head, heart and soul. The age when you first fell in love, perhaps. Or when you felt most carefree and alive. Certainly when it comes to the cooking and consumption of food, I'm still seventeen. Don't get me wrong, I adore fine food – a little too much sometimes – but as far as its preparation goes, I'm still basically a student. My watchwords are 'quick' and 'easy'. Even if I can now afford ingredients rather more advanced than baked beans and beef burgers that cost about 8p each, I still firmly belong to the "chuck it all in a pan and see what happens" school of cookery. When it comes to what I actually eat, my tastebuds are as preserved in aspic – or more accurately cumin, chilli and turmeric – as my mental age. Having spent my student years around the so-called 'Balti Belt' in Birmingham (which often meant eating three curries a day), I rarely enjoy anything that isn't spicy as all hell and believe that there is not a meal that has been invented that cannot be improved with liberal doses of Tabasco. I'll wallop it all over Weetabix given half a chance.

A Note On The Recipes Themselves

You will notice that aside from never using words such as "jus" or "coulis" I'm rather vague when it comes to measurements. I prefer to freewheel and have therefore abandoned traditional descriptions such as "a teaspoonful" and "a cup" while the actual use of weights and measures is jettisoned completely in favour of terms such as "some" and "a bit of". Hey, that's the way I roll. Though extremely anal – borderline OCD in fact – when it comes to the alphabetisation of books and CDs, I'm rather more slapdash when I'm given control of the kitchen. I'm tidy and firmly believe in washing up as you go along, but that's about as organised as it goes. While I apologise in advance to those mistakenly attempting to follow any of my recipes, my sympathy is limited as you would certainly be far better off with those that provide a little more guidance or indeed any degree of accuracy. There are some wonderful recipe ideas provided by others who appear to care rather more about how things turn out. Mine, on the other hand, are tailored for those who (A) can't really be bothered, (B) are unconcerned with appearance, or (C) have just staggered home drunk from the pub.

Complicated? No!

Tasty? You bet!

Suitable for that dinner party to impress your friends or loved ones? Er…

Cheese Slop

Now, I know this doesn't sound appetising, but you're going to have to trust me. This is merely the name given to this perennial favourite by my own family, but they're always happy enough to eat it. Is there cheese involved? Certainly. Is it sloppy? Well, that's entirely up to you…

Ingredients

A knob* of butter
Plain flour
Milk
Cheese (mature Cheddar is best)
Eggs (at least one per person)
Pasta. Any sort really. Fresh is best, I know, but it's not vital. Personally I'm a fan of the stuff that looks like tiny bow ties.
Bacon

I'm actually chuckling even as I type this. I'm far too juvenile to ever make a chef. I invariably giggle like a child if I see "shiitake" mushrooms on a menu.

Execution

Making the roux sauce is probably the most complicated part of this. OK, it's the only complicated part, but that's just me. You probably think that knocking up a roux sauce is easy. Well, why are you wasting your time reading this then, smartarse? Melt your butter, then add a little flour at a time, mixing it together until it starts to "ball" up. This is a culinary term of my own invention. When it does, start adding milk little by little until the ball starts to soften. You have to keep on stirring or your sauce will be lumpy and you might as well throw the whole lot away and send out for pizza. Once you've got a nice saucy sauce, thicken it by adding grated cheese, a fistful at a time. There you go, cheese sauce. Easy-cheesy!

While you're doing this, you should be hard-boiling your eggs and here's a handy tip – why not use the same boiling water to cook your pasta? I'm quite proud of that. Anyway… At the same time (and as with sex or joke-telling, timing is everything) you should be gently cooking your bacon, which you will previously have cut into bite-size pieces. Grill it, fry it, I don't really care. All tastes the same.

Once your pasta is cooked, you need to chop up your hard-boiled eggs and chuck them in. You can then chuck in your bacon. I'm starting to believe that "chuck" is a much undervalued word when it comes to cooking. It sounds like the kind of thing Jamie Oliver would say, doesn't it? Gordon Ramsay would almost certainly use it too, but he would be swearing a lot at the same time. "Chuck the bloody bastard thing in the f---ing saucepan, you bloody f---ing bastard." You get the idea…

Then it's time to pour in the cheese sauce and mix the whole lot together. Now, I know what you're thinking. This is basically pasta with a carbonara sauce, isn't it? Actually, it takes a little longer to make than a traditional carbonara (what with that fiendishly complicated roux and everything) and I prefer all the extra sauce you get with mine. Actually, I say that, but being as fond of sauce as I am of anything spicy, I DO tend to add a dollop or three of HP sauce to my cheese slop before eating it. Up to you, though.

Goes well with:

A fruity Sancerre.
Any Sauvignon Blanc that is innocent while not naïve.
Beer.

And why not try… Tuna Slop!:

A cunning variation on the basic "slop" format, but this time, you can use tinned tuna and mushrooms instead of eggs and bacon. Bloody gorgeous!

Spicy Stir-fry/Paella

This is the ideal dish for those wishing to utilise leftovers. You know, those vegetables you bought because you thought you should and are now rotting in that drawer at the bottom of the fridge. You can use pretty much anything you fancy with this one, though I would avoid fruit, nuts, or any meat that has gone green. If anything is a day or two past it's sell-by date, I wouldn't worry. There's enough chilli in this to cover a multitude of sins or potentially lethal bacteria. What follows is the "classic" recipe, though as with all great recipes, feel free to improvise.

Ingredients

Oil
Red chillis (several)
Mushrooms (not shitaake, because you'll be too busy laughing to concentrate)
Green peppers
Red peppers
Peppers of any colour
Chicken (cut into chunks)
Squid (cut into rings, though I actually prefer the bits with all the legs on)
Prawns
Green beans
Peas
Etc.

Execution

I favour the large wok with this one – the ideal container when it comes to "chucking" (see previous note). Heat up your oil (sesame, olive, rapeseed, motor, etc) then chuck in a finely copped chilli or two, the mushrooms, the chopped peppers and the chicken. You can add liberal dollops of hot sauce at any time. When the chicken has browned you can pretty much toss in the other stuff at will. You 'stir' and it 'fries'. You can see where this recipe got its clever name, can't you? Towards the end you can add your peas and chopped up green beans which, apart from being very healthy, make the thing look really nice and you know how important presentation is, right? Now, if you're on one of these faddy low-carb diets, you can just eat your spicy stir-fry as it is. However, if you've given up on all that because it's a waste of time and you'd rather eat chips and be a bit porky than have smelly breath, then why not throw in a bag of Uncle Ben's Spicy Mexican rice? Two minutes in the microwave, how good is that? Voila, spicy paella!

As with all my recipes, this is fantastic heated up a day or two later and you can keep adding things if you're a bit skint and need it to last the week.

Now, I don't want you to think that ALL my recipes are this straightforward. I have been known to spend upwards of twenty minutes knocking a meal together (though that did involve the shopping). Seriously... I do occasionally enjoy a day spent knocking up a moussaka (what is it with bloody aubergines?) or doing creative things with fish and freshly harvested roadkill. For the most part though, I don't have the time or the patience to get too tricksy and so I have, for the purposes of this anthology, concentrated on meal ideas that are quick and simple; recipes that quite frankly a chimp could master.

Enjoy!

BILLINGHAM'S TOP TIP:

Marmite makes almost everything better, with the possible exception of sex.

Tomato and Artichoke Risotto

Val McDermid

Serves 4

Ingredients

Olive oil
Butter
Generous handful of fresh sage
Arborio rice
Glass of red wine or dry vermouth
400g tin chopped plum tomatoes
400g tin artichoke hearts/jar of grilled artichoke hearts
Sun-dried tomato paste
Parmesan shavings

Execution

Melt a generous knob of butter in a tablespoon of olive oil in a large heavy pan over a medium heat. Coarsely chop the sage leaves and when the butter is bubbling, add to the pan. Stir till the leaves start to crisp then add two espresso cups of Arborio rice. Stir for a couple of minutes then add the red wine. Stir until the wine has completely reduced then add the tin of tomatoes. Stir till it reaches the boil. Drain the artichoke hearts and slice vertically into quarters. Add to the pan and stir through the rice mixture. Add two teaspoons of sun-dried tomato paste. As the rice absorbs the liquid, add water, an espresso cup at a time, until the rice is soft and cooked through. Allow the risotto to absorb the rest of the liquid till it is soft and slightly sticky. Season with salt to taste. Serve with Parmesan shavings scattered on top.

Veggie Haggis

Caro Ramsay

This is a good thing to make and not tell folk what it is! I make it in little circles like black pudding and it can be made to fit on a potato scone (see page 103). Haggis is like curry: you can mess about with the ingredients until you find the combination that suits you. I like peppery haggis with an oatmeal texture. I've also made this with veggie mince. The recipe is much the same, just omit some of carrots/mushrooms/kidney beans and put the veggie mince in instead, but make it twenty-four hours beforehand and let the flavours fuse a little. Veggie mince needs to absorb the flavour.

Crime writing tip: when dealing with a 400 page script, sometimes you want to mark a place in the narrative, or several places, to check continuity whenever the narrative returns to a recurring theme. Using a weird word and the 'find' function is a very useful tool. I use the word wombat (as it will never appear in any of my novels...). The word haggis would also be a good choice!

Serves about 4

Ingredients

1 tbsp sunflower oil
1 wee onion, finely chopped
50g carrots, finely chopped
35g mushrooms, chopped
50g red lentils
600ml vegetable stock or Marmite
25g tinned red kidney beans, mashed
35g peanuts, ground or finely chopped
25g ground hazelnuts
1 tbsp soy sauce (can be omitted if using Marmite)
1 tbsp lemon juice
2 tsp dried thyme
2 tsp dried rosemary
generous pinch cayenne pepper
2 tsp mixed spice
200g fine oatmeal (I like to use pin head)
1 tsp freshly ground black pepper (and the rest! I like more than this but it can be added later to taste)
Some sea salt to season

Execution

Stick the oven on (190°C). Put oil in a heavy-based pan with the onion. Cook until the onion is soft then add the carrot and mushrooms and cook for five minutes, then add the lentils and three quarters of the stock. Keep the remaining stock in a jug and stir in the mashed red kidney beans, then pour it into the pan with the nuts, soy sauce, lemon juice and seasonings. Cook this for another ten to fifteen minutes giving it a good stir every now and again. Then add the oatmeal, reduce heat, and simmer for fifteen to twenty minutes. You might need to add a little more stock if it starts to look dry. Leave to cool slightly then form into patties and bake on a lightly oiled baking tray for twenty minutes or so.

Ideally, this should be served with mashed neeps/swede/turnip, with a side order of gravy made from onion and Marmite!

SHONA MACLEAN

Like Shona, I've been a veggie for many years and so far no body parts have fallen off. I made these, just to check that Shona's recipe was right, of course, and then we sat in front of the tele and stuffed our faces. Highly recommended.

Caro

Veggie Chimichangas

I come from the kind of family that does not believe in pandering to what they see as pinko, work-shy sensibilities. One sibling's response to the news that I had written a book was, 'Will it be the kind of thing a normal person could read?' Vegetarianism comes under a similar heading to (alleged) novel-writing. Reactions to my eating habits range from, 'Aye, but you'll still eat chicken, surely?' to 'None of your turnip stew for me.' Well, here is a recipe that they all like - and believe me, they would have said if they didn't. It's easy, and doesn't take long. I make it a lot if we're having friends round, and serve it with rice and salad.

Serves 4

Ingredients

2 tbsp olive oil
1 onion, sliced
2 cloves garlic, chopped
1 or 2 sliced chillies, to taste
400g tin chopped tomatoes
2 tsp light muscovado sugar
3 handfuls of fresh coriander leaves
400g tin kidney beans
400g tin cannellini beans
About 10 flour tortillas
115g cheese, grated
300ml crème fraîche (less if preferred)

Execution

Preheat oven to 200°C. Heat the oil and fry the onion and garlic together for five minutes, then add the chillies and fry for another two.

Add the tomatoes, sugar and coriander. Stir and simmer for five minutes, then add both types of beans and stir through.

Put the tortillas side by side in a large baking/lasagne type dish. Spoon some mixture down the middle of each tortilla and roll them up.

Stir the grated cheese in to the crème fraîche and spread over the top and bake in the oven for twenty minutes.

Spiced Onion Tarts

A suitably medieval recipe which my detective, the fifteenth century lawyer Gil Cunningham, would have recognised and enjoyed. This is the original form, as found in A Forme of Cury, *the cookery book from Richard II's kitchens:*

Tarte in ymbre day. Take and perboile oynouns & erbes & presse out yhe water and hewe hem smale. Take grene chese & bray it in a morter, and temper it vp with eyren. Do yherto butter, saffroun & salt, & raisons corauns, & a litel sugur with powdour douce, & bake it in a trap, & serue it forth.

More edibly for the twenty-first century palate, you can leave out the currants and the sugar, but the spices make a surprising and tasty addition to an onion tart.

Ingredients

230g shortcrust pastry
450g onions
Butter for sweating the onions
Cloves, mace or nutmeg, ginger
Parsley
170g curd cheese
2 medium eggs
Salt and pepper
Milk or water if needed
A good handful of raisins if liked

Execution

Preheat the oven to 190°C. Line a flan tin or small pie tins with the shortcrust pastry (the bought chilled sort saves a lot of trouble).

Chop the onions. I find it helps to sweat them a little in butter or oil first; if you add the spices at this point it brings out the flavour well. While they are sweating, sprinkle over them a good pinch of cloves and mace or nutmeg, and also some powdered ginger if you like. Be cautious: the effect you are after is simply a warming of the flavour, rather than a curried pie.

Meanwhile, beat curd cheese (a well-known proprietary soft cheese, or cottage cheese, or any other soft cheese will do fine) with the eggs. Add a dash of milk or water if needed.

Remove the onions from the heat and stir in some chopped parsley, and the raisins if you are using them. Put the filling into the pastry case or cases, and cover with the egg and cheese mixture.

Bake for about thirty minutes (or about ten to fifteen minutes for tartlets).

Spiced Lentil Salsa

Peter James

This recipe was kindly provided to my by the Caprice Restaurant, London, for a dinner party I cooked and served as a challenge for The Guardian *newspaper: I had to do something I had never done before – which was to cook for an entire dinner party. It makes a fantastic accompaniment to poached salmon. Serve with a sprinkling of coriander and a rocket salad. Accompany with a sturdy, rich white wine, a Gewürztraminer or a big new world Chardonnay or an Albarino.*

Serves 6

Ingredients

2 medium red onions, peeled and finely chopped

90g ginger, peeled and finely chopped

4 cloves of garlic, peeled and crushed

4 medium chillies, seeded and finely chopped

2 tbsp ground cumin

2 tsp cumin seeds

150ml balsamic vinegar

100ml water

500g puy lentils, cooked

1 bunch coriander, finely chopped

120ml chilli sauce

120g sun-dried tomatoes, soaked and finely chopped

120g tomato ketchup

80ml sweet soy

100ml olive oil

Salt and freshly ground black pepper

Execution

Put the onions, ginger, garlic, chillies, ground cumin and seeds into a pan with the water and balsamic vinegar and simmer for two minutes with the lid on to release the flavours.

Remove from the heat and all the other ingredients, mix well and refrigerate overnight. Season and adjust if necessary. Can be served hot or cold on the day.

Omelette Nature

Peter James

There are all kinds of myths about the perfect omelette. In my view, after years of trial and error, this very simple way is the best! Just experiment until you get it as hard or soft as you prefer. In terms of a wine to go with it – forget it. I don't think any wine goes with eggs. English breakfast tea for me, every time!

Serves 1 (better to make these individually)

Ingredients

   2 large eggs, preferably free range
   Olive oil or groundnut oil
   Salt and freshly ground black pepper

Execution

Cover the base and sides of small non-stick frying pan with oil. Place on hob to get hot.

Break the eggs into a bowl, add salt and pepper, and beat with a fork for some moments, until properly blended.

Now tip into the frying pan.

Holding the pan, move the egg mix around, taking care not to brown the bottom. Use a wooden spatula to prevent the egg sticking to the sides. The side will cook faster, so keep curling the edges over. When the outside is starting to look done, while the inside is still undercooked, fold the outside over to cover. Leave on the heat for just a few moments, remembering it will continue to cook on the plate.

Tip from frying pan onto plate. Enjoy with hot buttered multi-grain toast or a wholemeal bagel.

Baking

JOHN LAWTON

John writes very fine literature crime fiction and I think is generally considered the man who will follow in John Le Carre's footsteps. He is also one of those men who can wear a linen suit very well – the crime writing equivalent of Bill Nighy.

He and I have had some great arguments, which I usually win. He then gets his revenge by emailing me from a sun-soaked villa somewhere in Tuscany and waxing lyrical about it as I sit in rain-drenched Glasgow.

Bread that Should Need Nowt On It

(This is in metric only because the measuring jug and the scales are in soddin' metric. I think in imperial and cannot be arsed to do the conversion.)

Ingredients

1 sachet instant yeast

1 tsp sugar

575-600g flour – a mixture of brown and white, roughly four to one

A handful of raisins

A handful of fresh rosemary leaves (grows like a weed - if you don't have it, steal it from someone's garden; it is said to be good for memory)

A pinch of chilli flakes

1 tbsp china tea leaves (preferably jasmine or gunpowder, but whatever it is it should be a big leaf)

1 heaped tsp sea salt

Big splash of olive oil

Big splash of cider vinegar (both of which are said to be good for the heart...)

Wee drop of balsamic goo

Dollop of black molasses or treacle (the metric for dollop is what exactly?)

320ml water

Optional: 1 onion and 6 cloves of garlic, sliced and fried until transparent

Execution

Bung the lot into a bread machine in the above order.

If machine is set to 'normal' or 'overnight' it tends to produce a denser loaf, as the dough has time to settle after its initial rise and never quite rises as high the second time, which is OK. Crunchy too. If you want fluffy, and fluffy can be overdone, set it to 'quick'.

CARO RAMSAY

My detective is always eating a fried egg and potato scone roll, which I have to confess, is my favourite meal. When I was at Uni in London, the two things I missed most about home were the dog and potato scones, and I used to get the latter posted down in food parcels.

Caro

Potato Scones

Potato scones are now found in quite posh restaurants, often as the ground floor of a stack of 'other stuff' – haggis, black pudding, ham, egg. Any food that has to be dismantled before you can eat it is best avoided!

These are best made in circles so that they fit the roll.

Ingredients

225g potatoes, boiled and mashed
3 tbsp melted butter
½ tsp salt
60g flour

Execution

While the potatoes are still warm, add the butter and salt and enough flour to make it like Play Doh. Dod this about. (Kneading? Bashing? Very therapeutic venting of anger.) Put it on a floured surface and roll out to a quarter-inch thick. A jam jar will do as a rolling pin if you can't find anything else. Cut into circles using the jam jar as a rough template. Prick the scones all over with a fork and cook in a heavy pan which has been lightly greased. Cook each side for about three minutes or until golden brown.

Variations:

Put melted cheese in between.
Eat warm with loads of butter and Marmite.
Eat cold with butter. With a nice cup of tea.
Once cooked and cooled these are good to freeze!

Lumber-Flapjack

My writing routine is strictly mornings only. I like to be out in my shed, pencil in hand, by eight-thirty. I write non-stop until my stomach lets me know it's about eleven.

Then I pop into the house, make a cup of tea, and before heading back to my shed, shove a slice of lumber-flapjack down my throat.

Aside from tasting damn good, I designed it to stave off hunger for as long as possible.

Ingredients

500g jumbo oat flakes (preferably Scottish, of course)
280g brown sugar (the darker, the better)
115g chopped dates
A handful of raisins
A handful of pumpkin seeds
A handful of sunflower seeds
340g margarine

Execution

Preheat the oven to 190°C.

Put everything but the margarine into a big bowl. Melt the margarine in a saucepan over a low heat then pour it into your lumber-flapjack mix and work it evenly through. I use my hands.

Transfer the mix into a large baking tray and smooth it down, then place in an oven for fifteen minutes or until the top is golden-brown.

Remove, allow to cool for five minutes, then score into squares while still warm. Allow to cool completely, then remove each (now hard) piece from tray. Enough for a score of man-size slices!

Maw Gray's Best Ever Recipe for Scones

Forensic tip: keep floor clear of spilt flour or your footprints will show up.

Ingredients

225g self-raising flour plus extra to dust
¼ tsp salt
1 tsp baking powder
40g butter, softened, plus extra to grease
About 150ml milk
1 medium egg, beaten

Execution

Preheat the oven to 220°C and grease a medium baking sheet. Sift the flour, salt and baking powder together into a bowl. Rub in the butter with your fingertips till it resembles fine breadcrumbs.

Stir in enough milk to make a soft dough. On a lightly floured surface flatten the dough with your hands to the thickness of one inch then use a cutter to stamp out rounds. Bring the trimmings together and reshape and stamp out more until all the dough is used. Make a wee one with any leftover. (There's always some annoying slimmer wanting a wee scone!)

Put the scones on the greased baking sheet and brush the tops with either the beaten egg or a few drops of milk. Bake for about ten minutes at the top of the oven till they are nice and golden. Serve while still warm with cream and sliced strawberries (yum!) or butter and home-made jam.

These scones freeze well.

DC Lisa Carmichael's Deadly Drizzle Cake

On page 348 of my debut novel, The Murder Wall, *DC Lisa Carmichael gets her auntie to make the tactical support group 'a nice lemon drizzle cake' to keep up their morale as they search for a vital piece of evidence in the hunt for a serial killer. It reappears again on page 46 of* Settled Blood, *the follow up which will be published in November 2012. I am now writing my fifth book in the Kate Daniels series and the cake – a one-time secret recipe – makes an appearance in all of them.*

Ingredients

170g self-raising flour
170g caster sugar
3 eggs
110g margarine
1 tbsp baking powder
Grated zest of 2 lemons
4 tbsp milk

Execution

Mix together and bake 180°C for one hour.

For the deadly drizzle:

Heat 110 grams of caster sugar with the juice from two lemons and drizzle over the top.

Sweet Things

FRANK MUIR

I would like to say that although this recipe makes Frankie sound like a health freak, every email I get from him ends with the phrase, 'nipping out for a pint now'... His detective is Andy Gilchrist, who spends much of his time thinking in pubs in and around St Andrews with a pint. I think Frankie takes his research very seriously.

Caro

Frankie-Fruitie

Let's get pithed!

The following recipe for a Frankie-Fruitie is a simple, cheap, mouth-refreshing, healthful breakfast or pudding for two, using only fresh, cleaned and sliced, fruit.

Serves 2

Ingredients

1 grapefruit
1 orange
1 melon
1 banana
Handful of strawberries/blueberries/raspberries/grapes, as preferred
1 lemon (optional)

Execution

The key to a successful Frankie-Fruitie is the direction in which the fruit is cut. Rather than cut the grapefruit and orange through the equator, half each of them from pole to pole. Take each of the sliced halves and carefully slice off segments, once again from pole to pole – aim for about six segments per half, depending on size – leaving the core of the fruit untouched, which can then be discarded.

Do the same with a whole melon, cutting it in half from pole to pole, leaving the pips intact. Take one of the halves, and half that again from pole to pole, leaving quarter of a melon. Scrape out pips, then carefully slice segments off the quarter melon from pole to pole, leaving slender juicy strips of melon. The remaining melon pieces – half melon and quarter melon – can be wrapped in cling-film (pips intact) and kept in the fridge for use in three more Frankie-Fruities.

Share the grapefruit, orange and melon slices between two side-plates, arranging the orange and grapefruit around the edge, and the melon in the middle.

Take one banana and slice it in two, this time across the equator – each half banana can be further sliced longwise, or through the middle, depending on personal preference – then add to side-plates.

Add two or three other fruits to the mix as preferred – strawberries (first cut the stem out of each strawberry by running a sharp blade around it, then pull out and discard), blueberries, raspberries, and seedless grapes (sneck the top off the grapes and discard). Place on side-plates with other fruit.

For those who like a real bite to their Frankie-fruitie, add a lemon – segmented once again from pole to pole, and shared by two. But be careful, this can put hairs on your chest.

After each citrus and melon segment is eaten, all that is left is the skin and some pith. So enjoy your breakfast for once, get pithed, and serve yourself and your loved one an original Frankie-Fruitie – only made in Scotland.

Brother Scott's Bourbon Bread & Butter Pudding
Stuart MacBride

I should point out that 'Brother Scott' isn't a monk, he's my actual brother, and this is a recipe I've stolen from his hairy little mind. Scott's been the head chef at the American Embassy in Dublin for years and years and years, so he really knows his food.

This is lovely made with French bread, or brioche, or if you're riding the Crazy Train, leftover fruit loaf. And as we're Scottish up here, the bourbon frequently gets swapped out for a slightly smoky whisky. If you're tempted to try that, for God's sake don't use Laphroaig or Talisker or anything heavily-peated like that, or your B&B pudding will taste like the underside of a burning tramp. For extra sweetness you could go for Glayva (double the quantity), but we're happy with a nice Dalwhinnie or a twelve-year-old Isle of Jura.

Ingredients for the pud

300ml full fat milk – not that insipid green-topped stuff
300ml single cream
1 vanilla pod
4 large free-range eggs
100g caster sugar
1 tbsp good bourbon (or whisky, or 2 tbsp Glayva)
1 tsp cinnamon
50g butter
About 16 thin slices of French bread (it really depends on how big your dish is)
85g raisins
50g pecans, roughly chopped

Ingredients for the sauce

1 tsp cornflour (or cornstarch if you're that way inclined)
150ml single cream
25g caster sugar
1 tbsp bourbon (or... etc, etc,...)

Execution

First off, preheat your oven to 180°C. Now butter a shallow ovenproof dish that's going to be big enough to fit all your bread. Next get yourself a pan and add the milk and cream. Split your vanilla pod and scrape out the seeds, then chop the pod and add the lot to the cream and milk. Heat gently until it's just boiling and no more, then take it off the heat, stick a lid on it, and leave everything to infuse for ten minutes.

Beat your eggs in a bowl and tip in the sugar. Whisk it together until it's pale and frothy, then – whisking all the time – add the strained warm creamy mixture. Don't lump it in all at once, and make sure you keep whisking, or you'll end up with watery sweet scrambled eggs. Finish off by glugging in the bourbon and half of the cinnamon and giving it a stir.

Butter the bread on both sides, then overlap them in the buttered dish with the crusts sticking up. Sprinkle the raisins on, then top everything off by straining the boozy custard over the bread. Leave it to all ooze together for ten minutes. Sprinkle the top with the nuts and what's left of the cinnamon, then bake in the oven until golden.

For the sauce:

Mix the cornflour into a tablespoon of the cream till it's smooth, then whisk it, and the sugar, into the rest of the cream in a pan. Cook over a medium heat until it thickens, then add the bourbon.

Serve the pudding hot, dusted with icing sugar (or chocolate chips) and slathered in sauce. Mmm...

White Chocolate and Whisky Bread and Butter Pudding

Peter James

As a type-2 diabetic, this dish is about as bad for me as it gets! But hey, if I am going to have a sugar hit, then I always make it a good one. And for extra measures, I break out a fine Sauternes from my cellar. A Beaumes De Venise also goes sinfully well with it!

Serves 6

Ingredients

500ml whole milk
500ml double cream
1 vanilla pod
3 whole eggs
5 egg yolks
200g caster sugar
1 loaf Warburton's (or similar) fruit bread
25g sultanas
25g butter, melted
175g white chocolate, grated
3 tbsp scotch whisky
50g apricot jam
Icing sugar
½ litre vanilla ice cream
1 tsp fresh mint

Execution

Preheat the oven to 200°C. Pour the milk and cream into a pan, add the vanilla pod, and slowly bring to the boil.

Place the eggs, egg yolks and sugar together in a food mixer with the whisk attachment and mix gently on a low setting (or you could do this by hand).

While the cream is heating, cut the bread slices in half and place in an ovenproof dish, slightly overlapping the pieces. Sprinkle with sultanas and pour over the butter.

Once the cream has boiled, take it off the heat. Add the egg mixture and white chocolate and stir well. Set to one side to allow the chocolate to melt, stirring continuously.

Add the whisky to the cream mixture. Next, using a sieve, strain the cream over the bread, cover with foil, and bake in the oven for fifteen to twenty minutes or until almost set.

Remove from the oven, brush the top with the jam and dust with icing sugar. Caramelize the topping using a very hot grill, or if you have one, a blow-torch.

Serve with ice cream and chopped fresh mint.

TONY BLACK

My and Tony's first foray with this project was Jenga chips! Buy chips from chippie, arrange them like Jenga - impress your guests. Eat. Then we settled for this: his sister's superb key lime pie.

Caro

Key Lime Pie

The apex of my culinary experimentation occurred somewhere around 1992 when I mastered the art of the Pot-Noodle. I was a student, so Pot-Noodle was in the contract. I think there might have been a brief dalliance with the ill-fated Pot-Rice, which the Spar down the road stocked, but in my heart I knew the Pot-Noodle was my true love. That and cereal. We had a phrase in my student digs: 'You can go a long way with a smile, but you'll go further with a smile and a Kellogg's Variety Pack.'

Last year my accountant chided me for trying to pass off a 'sustenance' expense double that of all my other expenses, so you can see I still haven't managed to cook. This recipe for key lime pie is actually stolen from my sister - whose kitchen, I hasten to add, contains not a single Pot-Noodle.

Ingredients

140g chocolate digestive crumbs

4 - 5 tbsp unsalted butter, melted

2 tbsp granulated white sugar

3 large egg yolks

400g can sweetened condensed milk

2 tsp grated lime zest

125ml key lime juice

250ml whipping cream

2 tbsp granulated white sugar

Execution

Preheat the oven to 170°C.

To make the chocolate digestive base, mix the crumbs, melted butter and sugar together. Press into the bottom and sides of a greased cake tin. Cover with cling-film and leave to chill.

While the crust is chilling beat the egg yolks with a mixer until frothy (about three minutes). Gradually add the condensed milk and beat for another four to five minutes until light and fluffy. Add the lime zest and lime juice, mix thoroughly.

Pour the filling into the chocolate digestive base and bake for ten minutes, or until the filling is set. Remove from oven and cool completely then refrigerate until ready to serve.

When you're ready to eat, prepare the topping by beating the whipping cream until soft peaks form. Add the sugar and beat until stiff peaks form.

Spread onto the pie and serve.

Raspberry Cranachan

Caro Ramsay

Anybody can make this and it looks very impressive served in posh wine glasses with long elegant spoons – just make sure that the spoon is long enough to get to the bottom of the glass. The real McCoy Cranachan can be a bit heavy after a full meal so I use whipping cream rather than double cream and sometimes Greek yoghurt instead of fromage frais. Any fruit will do and orange or cranberry juice can be used for the non-drinkers. I'm a non-drinker but pals say Drambuie really gives it a kick.

My friend made this in bulk, filled a load of wine glasses with it, and served it as a BBQ dessert to be eaten standing round the fire.

Serves 4

Ingredients

5 tbsp porridge oats, the rougher the better
150ml whipping cream
165g fromage frais
2 tbsp clear honey
2 tbsp whisky
400g raspberries

Execution

Toast the oats under the grill until they turn golden (about two to three minutes). Leave them to cool. Whip the cream and fromage frais together until thick. Then fold in the honey, whisky and four tablespoons of the toasted oats.

Save eight or twelve good looking raspberries for the decoration then layer the rest with the cream mixture in four wine glasses: start with the raspberries and end with the cream mixture. Decorate each one with the remaining oats and raspberries. It will keep in the fridge for about an hour before serving.

The General's Caramelised Kulfi

Val McDermid

Ingredients

400g tin condensed milk
1 mango, diced into very small cubes (or dried mango, slightly softened by simmering in a small amount of water for about five minutes)
Seeds from 6 cardamom pods, roasted and ground
1 generous handful of pistachios, toasted
1 generous handful of raisins, soaked overnight in your alcohol of choice
500ml double cream, softly whipped

Execution

Simmer the unopened tin of condensed milk in a pan of water for about three hours then allow to cool completely.

Mix the boiled condensed milk with the mango, powdered cardamom, pistachios and raisins, and fold in the whipped double cream. Put in an ice cream maker and churn. Alternatively, pour into a container and freeze, taking out every forty-five minutes and stirring vigorously to break up the ice crystals.

Chocolate Fudge Pudding

Ingredients for the pudding

25g margarine
110g caster sugar
1 egg
110g plain flour
1 level tsp baking powder
2 tbsp cocoa
A little milk

Ingredients for the sauce

110g brown or white sugar
2 tbsp cocoa
275ml water

Execution

Preheat your oven to 190°C. Cream the margarine and sugar then beat in the egg. Add flour, baking powder, cocoa and milk, and beat well. Put into a greased pudding bowl.

Bring all the sauce ingredients to the boil in a small saucepan. Stir until the sugar has melted, then let cool a little before pouring over the mixture in the bowl. Do not stir it in!

Bake for thirty to forty minutes, by which time the pudding should have raised, firm to touch, with the thick chocolate sauce below.

Mmmm, delicious, and equally scrummy when cold.

YRSA SIGURDARDOTTIR

Yrsa is a civil engineer by day, crime writer by night. She got inspiration for her third novel, Ashes to Dust, from her volcanic homeland. Imagine your house is destroyed by volcanic ash when you are a child. Imagine returning home to the newly excavated house as an adult to discover a severed head and various corpses in the cellar...
Better than that, imagine luminous jelly!

Caro

Electric Jelly

The below is what happens when engineers swap recipes.

I got this from a French dam engineer a few years ago. As with many great foods, it is French in origin. Despite this I do not think you will find it in Larousse Gastronomique. *However, I can vouch for it as it is guaranteed to make kids happy.*

Ingredients

2 packets of jelly (they don't need to be the same colour)
2 sets of mini Christmas lights (the ones that run on batteries)
A large mould of your choice

Execution

Make up the first packet of jelly following the directions on the packet. When done, use enough of the mix to fill half of the mould you have chosen. Place it in the refrigerator overnight or for long enough for it to almost or fully harden. Once it's set, place the Christmas lights on top of it - feel free to stick the bulbs into the hardened jelly so that they will stay still. Make sure that the battery packs are not inside the mould and also that they are empty of batteries at this stage. Now make up the second packet of jelly and, when it has cooled somewhat, fill up the mould with it, pouring it over the lights. Wrap the battery packs in paper towels and small sandwich bags to keep them dry, then put it all in the fridge overnight.

When the jelly has set, turn it out onto a plate (it can help to dunk the mould up to the brim into hot water in the sink, but if you do this make sure that the water doesn't rise above the edges and that the battery packs remain dry). Once the jelly is on the plate, put batteries into the battery pack and switch on. Voila! The jelly will light up from inside.

Engineering recommendation: this dish is better served in the evening than during the day due to the difference in ambient lighting.

NJ Cooper's Complete
Dinner Party Menu

N J COOPER

N J Cooper's latest novel featuring Karen Taylor and Will Hawkins is <u>Vengeance in Mind</u>. I know that she's an expert in the kitchen, so I'll let her get on with it...

Caro

N J Cooper's Complete Dinner Party Menu

My forensic psychologist, Karen Taylor, would never cook a proper meal for herself. She's tall, thin, preoccupied, and not particularly interested in food, except when she's under severe stress. Then she has a terrible tendency to succumb to thick white-bread sandwiches, stuffed with about half a pound of bacon, dripping with mayonnaise and tomatoes cooked in the bacon fat, washed down by deep glugs of Australian Shiraz.

Her bloke, neurosurgeon Will Hawkins, on the other hand, is a great foodie and infinitely more self-disciplined. One of his chief delights when he's pleased with her (which isn't always) is to let himself in to her flat early on a Saturday morning and cook some elaborate and delectable breakfast, so that she awakes to the scent of, for example, Poor Knights of Windsor.

In a yet-to-be written novel, they are having another couple round for dinner and sharing the cooking, a high-risk plan that will undoubtedly lead to tension – if not worse. They have taken care to choose an easy menu that shouldn't take much more than an hour and a half in total (apart from the pudding's setting time), so, unless he gives her too many orders or she spreads too much mess around the kitchen, there should be no actual blood shed.

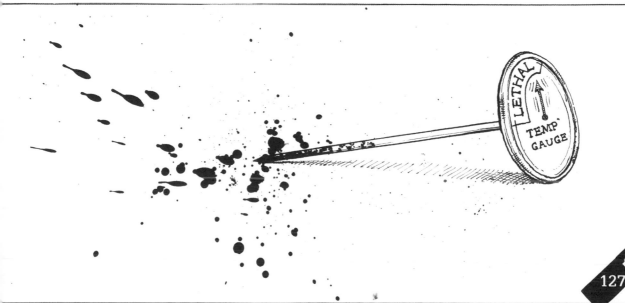

Tomato and Anchovy Bruschetta

Ingredients

1 sourdough loaf*
1 tin anchovies in olive oil, garlic and herbs
12 cherry tomatoes
2 buffalo mozzarella
Garlic
Olive oil

Will, of course, will have made his own bread, having kept his sourdough starter going for many years now. But most decent bakers can supply a good enough loaf. Just do not be tempted with pre-sliced packet stuff.

Execution

Cut four good slices from the loaf, nice and thick, and rub both sides with halved garlic cloves. Lay strips of anchovy across each slice, sharing the tin between the slices. Top with sliced mozzarella and then the cherry tomatoes, cut into thirds. (If you grow your own full-sized tomatoes or have access to a supply of tomatoes that taste of something, then you can use those. If not, cherry tomatoes are safer.)

Generously oil a baking sheet. Lay the bruschetta on it (cheese and tomato side up, obviously), drizzle more olive oil over the top of each piece and generously pepper it. You shouldn't need salt because of the anchovies. Bake at the top of the oven, above the chicken (see below), for about twenty minutes, until the mozzarella is melted and the bread is crisp.

This simple dish depends entirely on the quality of the ingredients: good and it's delicious; bog-standard and it's dull.

Roast Chicken and Potatoes with Garlic and Tarragon

Ingredients

1 large, free-range, organic chicken – or 8 chicken pieces
1kg Anya potatoes
2 unwaxed lemons
2 large onions
8 cloves of garlic
2 glasses dry white wine
Fresh tarragon

Execution

Preheat the oven to 200°C.

Joint the chicken, keeping the skin on and the bones in the thighs, drumsticks, and wings.

Wash the Anya potatoes and cut in half lengthwise. (You may not need the whole lot – it all depends on the size of your roasting tin.)

Wash the lemons and cut into eight wedges.

Peel the onions and cut into eight wedges.

Lay the chicken pieces in a single layer in a large roasting tin*, interspersed with pieces of onion and lemon and the whole, unpeeled, garlic cloves. Strip the tarragon leaves from the stalks and spread over the chicken, using as much or as little as your own taste demands. (Will likes a lot.) Place the halved potatoes between, around, and, cut-side up, on top of the chicken, without covering it completely.

Pour the wine over everything, season with Maldon salt and black pepper and cook in the oven for at least an hour, until the chicken is cooked through (the juices should run clear when the chicken is pierced with the point of a knife at the thickest part), its skin crisping and the potatoes caramelising at the edges. Check progress at intervals and, if everything looks as though it's drying out, add more wine, or, if you feeling skint, a little chicken stock, but do not drown it. It's important the skin and potatoes have a chance to crisp. Serve from the tin. The lemony-vinous-herby juices will provide the only sauce you will need. Accompany with plain green beans, or salad, if you prefer.

Will himself would never serve anything from any kind of pan and so he will try to make Karen cook these in an elegant ovenproof porcelain gratin dish. I prefer the heat-conducting properties of metal.

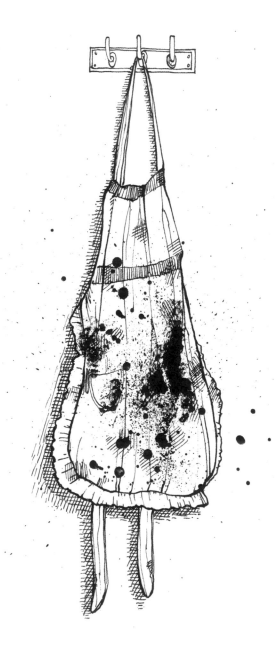

White Chocolate and Blackcurrant Pudding

Ingredients

250g good quality white chocolate (e.g. Green & Black's)
500g full fat crème fraîche d'Isigny
500g fresh blackcurrants (or the equivalent from your freezer)

Execution

Strip the blackcurrants from their stalks and cook gently with a little sugar until softened but not mushy. Do not overdo the sugar because the blackcurrants need to be tart. Set aside to cool. Melt the white chocolate over simmering water, taking care not to let the water touch the base of the bowl. When it's melted, stir it into the crème fraîche, making sure the two ingredients are fully amalgamated. Pour into four attractive glasses and refrigerate to set. I usually allow this to set overnight, but it shouldn't take more than a few hours. Just before you serve it, add a top dressing of the blackcurrant compote to each glass.

The same white wine should work with all three dishes, provided it has some body. Or you could have a medium-bodied red with the first two courses and a delicious Muscat with the pudding, although that will exaggerate the sharpness of the blackcurrant compote.

Done!

CHEF'S EMERGENCY EXIT

Index